PRACTICE DEVELOPMENT—
A GUIDE TO
MARKETING TECHNIQUES FOR ACCOUNTANTS

ACKNOWLEDGMENTS

We would like to thank our colleagues at Streets Financial for all their advice, assistance and encouragement. Our thanks are also due to John Trench for his help and support as well as to *The Accountant* magazine and CIPA Marketing Report.

PRACTICE DEVELOPMENT— A GUIDE TO MARKETING TECHNIQUES FOR ACCOUNTANTS

Simon Cowley
FCA, MIPA

Toby Mountford
BA, ACA

London
Butterworths
1984

England	Butterworth & Co (Publishers) Ltd, 88 Kingsway, LONDON WC2B 6AB
Australia	Butterworths Pty Ltd, SYDNEY, MELBOURNE, BRISBANE, ADELAIDE, PERTH, CANBERRA and HOBART
Canada	Butterworth & Co (Canada) Ltd, TORONTO and VANCOUVER
New Zealand	Butterworths of New Zealand Ltd, WELLINGTON and AUCKLAND
Singapore	Butterworth & Co (Asia) Pte Ltd, SINGAPORE
South Africa	Butterworth Publishers (Pty) Ltd, DURBAN and PRETORIA
USA	Butterworth Legal Publishers, ST PAUL, Minnesota, SEATTLE, Washington, BOSTON, Massachusetts, AUSTIN, Texas and D & S Publishers, CLEARWATER, Florida

British Library Cataloguing in Publication Data

Cowley, Simon
Practice development: a guide to marketing techniques for accountants.
1. Marketing
I. Title II. Mountford, Toby
658.8'024657 HF5415

ISBN 0-406-26040-0

Phototypeset by Cotswold Typesetting Ltd, Gloucester
and printed in Great Britain by Billings Bookplan, Worcester

CONTENTS

LIST OF FIGURES

Chapter 1

NEW FREEDOM—OR NEW THREAT?

The bounds of the permissible have been dramatically extended for accountancy firms that wish to use advertising for practice development, and the reactions of individual accountants range from downright opposition to exhilaration. Commoner than either is probably perplexity—a consciousness that the profession is standing on the edge of an unknown continent, and a fear that in crossing it some will lose their way and some be left behind.

It is the purpose of this book to dispel the perplexity. We offer a map of the land that lies ahead; we shall put up signposts and point out well-trodden ways that others have followed—and also a number of quagmires and precipices. In doing so we shall show that the opposition is unfounded, and that the exhilaration may be short-lived unless it is guided and disciplined.

We show that practice development—our equivalent of marketing—does not have to be the preserve of the large firms. Properly planned and professionally carried out, it is within the scope of even the sole practitioner. We show that effective advertising does not have to involve razzmatazz and ballyhoo, and we suggest that a regard for professional ethics can actually produce better advertising than would result from casting them aside.

We point out the practical steps that you can take to define your approach and follow it through to success, and we give you some objective yardsticks by which to judge any proposals that may be put before you.

What are the new rules?

The revised rules remove all restrictions on publicity and advertising, subject to an overall requirement of responsibility to the profession and the public interest. Specifically this means that cold calling and direct mail are *not* permitted, and requires members to ensure that material does not mislead, does not make derogatory comparisons with other firms' services (whether they are accountants or not), does not make claims that cannot be substantiated and does not offend against good taste. The ban on direct mail applies as much to newly formed companies, which, consequently, have no accountants, as to established companies who are already someone else's clients. It does not, of course, apply to your existing clients. The only other exceptions are that you may draw your services to the attention of other providers of financial services in your locality; and invite them, and holders of public office to specific events of relevance to the community they serve.

There is a size limit on the space you may take in the newspapers. A quarter page is the most any firm may buy in any one issue, and if associates or subsidiaries advertise in the same issue, the aggregate must not exceed a quarter page. This limitation does not apply in magazines or journals.

The surviving limitations have yet to be tested in practice, and there could be room for disagreement over their interpretation and application. It would be prudent to clear any proposals with the relevant committee of your professional body at an early stage.

Where do we, the authors, stand on this?

It may be possible to be neutral on an issue like this, but since neutrality is unlikely to produce a more useful book, we have not tried. Our position is that we think freedom to advertise can do nothing but good to the profession as a whole—provided the new rules are firmly and impartially applied.

The whole commercial world in which accountants operate has changed and continues to change. If change is resisted, accountants risk being left on the shore of history, a magnificent crumbling irrelevance. We all have to make ourselves and our services better known to the general public or they will increasingly look elsewhere for what they need. Accountants can no longer rely for their livelihood on their statutory monopoly of audit.

It has been said that the market growth from which all practices have benefited has now come to an end. We doubt this. That advertising generates market growth has been proved again and again in other fields, and growth is greater when the market is full of *competitive* advertising.

It has been said, too, that advertising will mean the end of professionalism. This we strongly rebut. It is a fear that arises, we believe, from a misunderstanding about the nature of advertising and how it works. Advertising that conflicts with people's idea of how an accountant ought to behave will rebound on the advertiser's head. Sir Gordon Borrie at the Office of Fair Trading is on record as wishing us to preserve all that is best from our past, which must surely include our traditional system of ethics; and we believe he is right in thinking this possible.

One other thing should perhaps be said. High standards of professional ethics are not in the least incompatible with low standards of professional competence. A world in which advertising is allowed is one in which the incompetent have less chance to survive and discredit the rest of us.

Chapter 2

IT DEPENDS WHAT YOU MEAN BY PRACTICE DEVELOPMENT

All advertising is going to be done with practice development in mind—even recruitment advertising; for what is recruitment but a means of developing your practice? So it is well to begin with a definition of practice development, and since it is agreed to be the accountant's equivalent of marketing, let us see how the Institute of Marketing defines that activity.

It is, says the Institute, the management process responsible for identifying, anticipating and satisfying consumer requirements profitably. For 'consumer' read 'client', and you have a definition of practice development. The firm that fails in this is going to fail, full stop.

Note that according to this definition, the old approach to selling one's services was not really marketing at all. It involved little effort to identify or anticipate client needs. One had certain skills, and if a client felt that those skills would meet his needs, he came to you. So long as there was a broad correspondence between his needs and your skills, this worked reasonably well. In other fields it led to what is called 'product/service orientation' in selling and advertising: the quality of whatever you had to offer was all it was necessary to communicate; the world was then expected to beat a path to one's door. And for a long time it did.

Marketing, as now understood, has a client/customer orientation. It involves considerable effort being devoted to finding what clients' needs really are and how they are changing, to identifying significant shifts in those needs and developing the ability to meet them *before* they leave you behind. It involves looking at the market—including yourself—from the clients' point of view, and humbly accepting *the clients'* perceptions of it as the determinant of all you do.

It is not only product/service development that has to be looked at from this marketing standpoint. Pricing is also part of the marketing mix—in accountancy terms, the setting of fee levels so that they are both competitive and profitable, and all this has to be communicated to existing and prospective clients in such a way that they are motivated at least to explore what your services have to offer. This is the role of publicity. (We are not forgetting personal salesmanship, but this manual is concerned with publicity.)

Professional advice is on a rather different footing. It is, of course, one of the services you offer, and may well be an important element in your relationship with some of your clients. Nothing we have said should be taken as implying that you should tell them only what they want to hear, and many will feel that even to mention it in advertising is at odds with the discretion and confidentiality that lie at its heart. Nevertheless, it is legitimate to choose the areas in which you offer advice in the light of your overall marketing objectives.

'Publicity? That's the same as advertising, isn't it?'

There are many possible ways of spreading the word about your firm and its services, and advertising is only one of them. Publicity is the most generally accepted blanket term for all of them, and it is not, therefore, the same as advertising. It includes also print, public relations, sponsorship, exhibitions and sales promotion.

The term '*advertising*' is best restricted to that form of publicity that involves the buying of newspaper space or air-time, or the hiring of poster sites, and using them to carry the advertiser's message. It thus covers newspaper and magazine advertisements, television and radio commercials, and the posters, bus-sides, tube-cards and taxi-panels that are comprised in the term 'outdoor' advertising.

Obviously many of these involve various printing processes. The term '*print*', however, is generally used to mean printed communication, entirely under the control of the advertiser, that does *not* reach the public through *paid-for* space in the media. Booklets, leaflets, folders, and direct-mail letters are all 'print'. So is what is known as 'point-of-sale material'—counter-cards, window-stickers and other printed material seen in shops, bank branches and building-society offices. Your own everyday company letter-head is 'print' too: it is just as much 'printed communication' as your corporate brochure.

Priceless—but you can't control it in detail

Much of the activity that comes under the heading of *public relations* also involves printed communication that is not in paid-for space. The difference is that since it appears in the editorial columns of the newspapers, advertisers have much less control over its content. You will hear stories about advertisers trying to bring pressure to bear on editors, and some of them are true. Some years ago a cinema chain withheld advertising from a national newspaper because the newspaper had published an adverse review. In that case, and in most others, the advertiser eventually found that he needed the newspaper more than the newspaper needed him. On the whole the press is seen as being impartial, and on the whole it deserves its reputation—which is what makes an inch of editorial worth ten inches of advertising.

Other public relations activities are the organisation of seminars and conferences, the production of reports, forecasts and manuals, and arranging television appearances for a firm's principals.

There are two basic kinds of public relations—the active and the reactive. Reactive PR produces considered responses to outside events, or reports and explanations of your own corporate activities and decisions, in line with the firm's policy. Active PR generates newsworthy activities and utterances within the company, for the sake of their PR value.

Sponsorship can legitimately be seen as an aspect of PR, and is generally initiated by a company's PR staff or its PR consultants. It tends to be thought of in terms of sport: a sponsor underwrites a sporting event, or puts up the prizes, or both, but it can just as well be, and very often is, applied to University Chairs, art exhibitions, concerts, chess tournaments, crossword contests or book publication. It produces a lot of publicity, but it is mainly 'name publicity' only: it gets the name of the advertiser before the public, but very little else. It is only by the choice of what to sponsor that the advertiser can convey any message about himself or his company: 'This is the sort of thing we care about. That shows you the sort of company we are.'

Exhibitions have always been important in some businesses, and are tending to proliferate. They are obviously mainly useful to companies who have something visible, tangible and demonstrable to offer.

Finally, sales promotion covers such activities as competitions, in-store demonstrations, premium offers, money-off promotions and store-openings by celebrities. You may think that neither sales promotion nor exhibitions have much to offer to accountancy firms. If so, we agree with you, though local societies might derive some benefit from a stand at the county show, for example. The London Society of Chartered Accountants had a successful stand at the 1983 Ideal Home Exhibition; there were a large number of enquiries, and much interest was shown.

Chapter 3

GETTING THE BASICS RIGHT

It is in practice impossible to draw hard and fast lines between the various kinds of publicity. They are not mutually exclusive, and cannot be considered in isolation from one another.

Print is often lumped together with advertising, and is generally designed, written and produced by the advertising agency. It is sometimes distinguished from media advertising by the term 'below-the-line' (in allusion to the way the budget is set out), which also covers sales promotion. PR merges into print in some of its aspects, as is shown by the fact that some PR consultancies offer a design service. Sponsorship, as we have noted, can be seen as a special kind of PR.

An indication of the intimate conceptual links between all forms of publicity is that in the last section we found it impossible to avoid using the word 'advertiser' to denote the person or organisation using PR, print and sponsorship. Publicity, in fact, is a seamless unity, but it involves many different skills, and is consequently a team effort. It is necessary to make sure that the whole team always pulls in the same direction.

What this means in practice is that every facet of your publicity must reflect a single coherent, positive, deliberate policy: and it must be a *marketing* policy. It is essential to be single-minded, to make sure that every time you 'interface' with the public (to borrow a useful bit of computer-speak), the public gets a consistent impression of you.

It is vital to remember all the time that you cannot do or say or write anything that the public is going to see or hear without conveying *some* impression of yourself. Everything is communication; and there is no such thing as non-committal communication.

Consequently it is necessary to arrive at a marketing strategy before you embark on any publicity of any kind; and then to make sure that all your communication conforms to it. The second part of that injunction can be more difficult to carry out than the first.

What do you want to achieve?

Before you can evolve a strategy you need to decide your objectives; and the starting point for this is provided by your *financial* objectives. Financial objectives are not the same as marketing objectives. The former are concerned with revenue, expenditure and profits; the latter with the means by which you maximise the revenue and the profits—what you must actually achieve in the market place.

A statement of what you hope to achieve in the market place can be no more than a hope or a guess unless you look carefully at your firm *in its market setting*. You need to produce an objective analysis of the firm's strengths and weaknesses, and of the threats and opportunities presented by the market—which includes not only clients and potential clients, but your competitors as well.

'Know thyself'

You will need to analyse your client list and compare it with the composition of the market. How many are in growth industries? How many are, in your terms, large or small? A distribution curve, showing numbers of clients by size, can be a useful tool: deviations from the 'normal' curve could be a danger signal.

You will need to analyse your services and see how they relate to the needs of the market. Are you satisfied that you know what those needs are? If so, is your satisfaction justified? Does it rest on objective, statistically valid data? How do your services compare with the competition? Are you, perhaps, trying to do too much?

Then there is the matter of fees. How does your fee structure measure up against the competition? What do your clients think of it?

What, indeed, do your clients think about the firm in general? Have you adequate means of finding out? Are your contacts the best you could have in each client company? Are you communicating the right things, in the right way, to the right people?

What about the quality of your people? Are their communication skills adequate? Are they marketing-minded? Motivated to sell, and equipped with the knowledge and ability and personality to do it successfully?

Your internal structure must come under scrutiny. Is it adapted for successful marketing, with clear responsibilities and clear chains of command? Does everybody know what they are supposed to be achieving, and how to measure their performance?

Where are you going?

Equipped with this knowledge, you are in a position to decide what marketing objectives it makes sense for you to aim at—what will do most towards achieving your financial goals, and what is realistically attainable. Without such an analysis you are groping in the dark.

All possible marketing objectives are variations or combinations of three basic aims. You can aim to:

increase your share of the existing market (which can be done only by taking clients from other firms)

expand the total market, or

improve the profitability of your existing operations.

The second of these—expanding the total market—can be further subdivided. You can:

expand your existing market (by selling more of your existing services to your existing clients)

develop new services for your existing market

develop new services for new markets (ie diversify)

find new markets for existing services (ie where no such services are at present used at all).

For achieving each objective there is a range of possible strategies, and your choice of objective will be partly governed by the availability of appropriate strategies. It is no good choosing an objective if you lack the means to attain it. Your analysis of your strengths and weaknesses will help you to see which strategies you can adopt, and consequently what objectives you can realistically hope to achieve. Alternatively, of course, it will identify the areas in which you need to strengthen yourself before you can embark on any particular strategy and hope to attain the desired goal.

How are you going to get there?

Having a formally defined strategy helps you to concentrate your efforts where they will be most fruitful. It encourages you to be single-minded, and not dissipate your resources on side shows.

To increase your market share, possible strategies include: concentrating resources against selected segments of the market; forming specialist units to attack particular segments; moving in on segments you have not served before; or across-the-board enhancement of services to broaden their appeal.

To expand your existing market you can get clients to use your services more often, or you can persuade them to use services that they do not use at present. Opening new offices might be a strategy that would contribute to this.

To develop new services for your existing market might involve no more than enhancing existing services. Developing radically new services, for example, by introducing a computer system or a consultancy service, obviously involves very much greater expense.

To develop new services for new markets you can build on your in-house strengths and abilities; you can acquire the strength you lack by merger or take-over; you could exploit the new technology, for example by developing software for management-information systems (this is likely to involve acquiring new strengths by hiring new people).

To find new markets for existing services can come to the same thing as increasing your market share, unless you can find a market, or part of the market, not at present served by anyone. This is perfectly possible. New businesses are being formed all the time—168,390 in 1983—and new individuals are finding themselves in need of accountancy services—whether they know it or not. Another possible field for expansion lies overseas.

To improve profitability (assuming there is no obvious scope for reducing overheads or for straight fee increases), possible strategies include: to enhance the perceived value of the services given to particular clients, or to reduce the range of services you offer. In any case it is worthwhile to analyse your own productivity and the contribution of each activity and each client to revenue and costs.

It is of course possible to combine a number of these strategies, but remember that the best strategic plans are the simple ones. If you try to do too much you diffuse your effort.

This analysis shows the essential difference between an objective and a strategy: a strategy is a course of action; an objective is the result you intend from that action. Confusing ends and means is a classic recipe for confused thinking, and is commoner than you might think.

Coming down to particulars

Strategy lays down broad lines of action. Its detailed application to particular circumstances constitutes tactics. When we talk about pursuing strategies with determination and single-mindedness, we are talking about how you conduct the tactics; it is only in tactics that strategy assumes any reality. It is in the tactical planning and execution that much painstaking strategic planning comes to grief.

In our discussion of possible strategies, the words 'services' and 'markets' occur constantly. Tactical planning means reaching firm, specific decisions about *which* services you mean to offer to which markets, or segments of the market. Each decision must reflect the chosen strategy, or the result is unlikely to be what you intend.

The profession as a whole has a 'captive' market in those organisations that are required by law to produce audited accounts. Audit is our bread and butter. Do we take it too much for granted? Do you take too limited a view of your relationship with your audit clients?

Looking closely at this relationship is one possible starting point for tactical planning. Is there scope for selling your audit clients other services? Would they welcome advice on corporate finance, for example? Many smaller companies could well prefer to come to you than to approach a merchant bank. They know you, and you know them and their system. This could be a useful diversification, and not too difficult to effect.

Do you know enough about your existing clients?

As a general rule it is best to consider first whether you can sell more services to existing clients, rather than go out and find new ones. It is generally easier and a great deal cheaper; and the more you do for a client, the firmer your relationship. You cannot begin to do this unless you know a great deal about your clients' businesses—more, in fact than is known by many accountants. They know all about sales figures, profits, balance sheets, and the results of subsidiaries, but they are often surprisingly ignorant about the product range, the distribution chain, who the customers are, the strength and nature of the competition, or the client's standing in the industry. Armed with this kind of information, you will be in a far better position to spot opportunities for additional business, either with the client or with people the client deals with. It is worth taking some trouble to draw up a detailed client profile, showing everything there is to be known about his business. Even if it wins you no more business, it will increase your client's confidence in you.

If you can broaden the work you do for existing clients, it will give you a base on which to build when you go looking for new clients for the services you have developed. These may well be other people's audit clients; you are not trying to oust the present incumbents from their audit business, but simply to move into gaps that they have left.

You must of course consider, in the light of your strategic plan, what *kind* of client you want to cultivate, whether among your existing list or in the market outside.

Matching capabilities to needs

Potential clients can be classified in several ways: by size—large, medium or small; by the business they are in—manufacturing, service, primary products, chemicals, engineering, construction, catering, retail and so on; by whether they are in the public or in the private sector; limited companies, subsidiaries, partnerships, or sole traders; new or established; by whether they are in a growth sector or a declining or static one. Do not forget private individuals.

According to how you classify them they will be seen to have different needs and present different opportunities.

How do your capabilities match the needs of the various possible classifications? Draw up a list of what you can offer, or might offer if you developed the ability, and match it to possible target groups. The following list is not intended to be exhaustive, but simply to start you thinking. It excludes audit, because that is where we suggest you start.

Advice on setting up companies, and their capital structure; or on reorganisation or reconstruction

Help with preparing prospectuses

Advice on sources of finance

Preparation of financial statements

Evaluation of new projects

Viability studies

Investigating companies for merger or take-over

Share valuations

Advice on forecasting

Advice on Government and EEC aid

Applying EEC Directives, especially 4 (Companies Act 1981) and 7

Investigations on behalf of the Department of Trade and Industry

Interpreting new legislation

'Value for money' audits for local authorities

Advice on information systems, including choice of computer system

Inflation accounting

Design and evaluation of accounting systems, formulating accounting policies and maintaining accounting standards

Exchange control

Accountancy for trusts and pension funds

Insolvency

Tax—a whole field in itself, including:

—help in reaching tax-effective decisions
—preparing returns
—VAT
—tax implications of employee remuneration, including share options
—problems arising from mergers or liquidations
—advice on capital taxes
—special taxes: petroleum, 'windfall', stamp duty, development land tax
—an up-date service on tax changes, judicial decisions and Inland Revenue rulings
—International tax

Services to smaller business, especially those managed by their owners:

—how to set up a business, what books to keep and how to keep them
—planning expansion
—managing cash-flow
—management information
—forecasting
—coming to the USM
—advice on whether to lease or buy equipment
—choosing a computer
—protecting the financial position of directors and their families

Services to prosperous individuals:
—advice on minimising tax
—preparing tax returns
—financial planning in general
—tax services for overseas residents in the UK.

You will want to build on your strengths, so you should consider if there is any area in which you have particular expertise, or have a comparatively large share of the market—local or national. If, however, you enjoy a high market share in a static or declining market, it could make sense to reinforce your effort elsewhere—where you have a small share of a growth market, for example.

At this stage you should also consider your fee structure. Is there further room for flexibility, for example by differential pricing according to who does the work, or to take advantage of special circumstances? How much scope would there be for fee increases if you were to enlarge the package of services for any particular client, in any of the ways suggested above?

How research can help

Success depends on the accuracy with which you match what you offer to what a segment of the market needs. But which comes first? Do you start with your services, and find clients that want them? Or do you start with the market segment that seems to offer most opportunity, find out what it wants and then set about gearing yourself up to provide it?

You will not wish either to make a clean sweep of existing services, nor to discard the new business potential of existing clients. So the answer is that you will probably have to start from both ends, and find a convergence. In either case you will need deep and extensive knowledge of the market.

You may well feel that you have this already. You have your ear to the ground; you can gauge business sentiment as well as anybody. You *know*—you may think—what the market is looking for, and you may well be right.

It is, however, surprisingly easy to be expensively wrong. Your contacts may be out of touch; they are almost certain to be unrepresentative; you may not be asking the right questions, and if you are, you may be getting lazy answers. Besides, one of the things you should be exploring is the possibility of entering *new* sectors of the market, where you do *not* have your ear to the ground.

Research can tell you what clients and potential clients are looking for, not only in the matter of services (where indeed common sense and market knowledge should be able to help you), but in the matter of *service*—all those qualities that can be defined only by abstract nouns: reliability, promptitude, accessibility of principals, judgment, rectitude, friendliness. It can tell you what kind of firm they like to deal with, and what kind of people. It can tell you about clients' attitudes to fees, their perceptions of what constitutes value for money, and whether there are 'fee-barriers' in their minds that would make it difficult for you to increase revenue.

All these things you will need to know before you can start to put together a programme of publicity, and the imponderables are at least as important as the concrete factors.

Large scale surveys in the mass market can be very expensive—but we are not talking about a mass market, and mass interviewing is not the only way of getting information. Other techniques—group discussions, postal surveys, telephone surveys—can also yield reliable results, and are comparatively cheap.

The only proviso is that this is not a do-it-yourself activity. Constructing questionnaires, selecting samples and conducting interviews are highly specialized and skilled activities, and it is essential to employ a professional market research consultancy.

If you are not contemplating spending very large sums on publicity, you may not be risking very much if you rely on your own 'feel' for the market, plus the judgment and expertise of your marketing consultants or advertising agency. If there are large sums at stake, or if you find yourself in fundamental disagreement with your advisers, it is likely to be false economy to grudge the money spent on market research.

How do you want to be seen?

So far in this chapter we have been talking about marketing, and, since this is not a manual of marketing, we have been using the broadest of brush strokes. Our aim has been simply to give you some idea of the planning that has to be done before you can usefully undertake any kind of publicity.

When you have done this planning you will know what you are going to sell, at what price, and to whom. You will also know what your intended market is looking for in its accountants.

You can now take the first step into advertising: defining, as explicitly as possible, the kind of firm you want the market to see in you. This constitutes your 'image'. The way it is defined is sometimes called a 'positioning statement'.

Do you, for example, want to be seen as a big, medium or small firm? The brute physical facts cannot, obviously be ignored: a big firm cannot make itself out to be small, but it could well happen that the market segment in which you have chosen to expand sees medium-sized firms as being best suited to its needs. In that case you would—if you were very big—avoid boasting about your size. A small one, on the other hand, might try to make the most of its size. Or it might decide to go after a market sector in which small size is seen as a virtue—because, for example, it is felt to indicate that the partners will be more accessible, or that you will pay more attention to their needs.

You might position yourself as the right firm for small businesses, or charities, or insurance companies; for tax advice or liquidations or computer software. You will obviously stress the skills that are most relevant to the range of services you are promoting—or rather, you will stress the benefits that flow from these skills. You will try to ensure that nothing in anything you write or do is at odds with the reputation you want to build—for efficiency, or ability to communicate with non-accountants, or authority. You may want to be seen as innovative, or you may deliberately cultivate an old-fashioned image. Decide, too, what your position is to be on controversial issues. Where do you stand on inflation accounting? What do you consider the correct way of valuing stock and work in progress?

It is a good idea to set your positioning statement down in writing. Then everything you do in the way of publicity can be measured against it. And you will always project the same personality: the right one.

Chapter 4

IDENTIFYING YOURSELF

When someone answers the telephone he does two things. He announces his identity, and—whether he intends to or not—he says something about himself as a person. He will do this by his tone of voice. Simply by uttering his name he will convey friendliness or hostility, confidence or diffidence, efficiency or vagueness. If he has been trained in the use of the telephone, the impression he gives will be the one he intends, but there is no way in which he can give *no* impression of himself.

In any written or printed communication that emerges from your firm—advertisement or letter, booklet or invoice—you have to announce your identity. The way you do this says as much about the firm as a man's voice on the telephone says about him. The printed equivalent of tone of voice is *typography*: the choice of typeface for your name, the spaces between the letters, and those between the words, and the size of your name in relation to other elements.

There are many hundreds of different type-faces, and they all have slightly different characteristics. They subtly modify the words for which they are used. Look at *Figure 1* and ask yourself which name is fuddy-duddy, which *avant-garde*, which mannered, which precious, which reliable. They are all the same name, but they say very different things about the owner of the name.

Type can be likened to clothes, as well as to tone of voice. It is clothing for words, and, like clothes, it is subject to fashion. It is good advice not to follow the latest fashion in type; it will very soon look old fashioned. You are safer if you adopt one of the timeless, classic typefaces. Brief your designer accordingly.

Similarly, avoid very mannered, self-conscious faces. Try not to provoke the question, 'What are they trying to prove?'.

Smith Jones & Co

Smith Jones & Co

Smith Jones & Co

Smith Jones & Co

SMITH JONES & CO

Smith Jones & Co

Smith Jones & Co

Smith Jones & Co

Figure 1 How you display your name in print can profoundly affect people's perception of your character.

What price symbols?

Some people go further than choosing a typeface in which to display their name. They seek a graphic, non-verbal expression of their identity as well; sometimes, if they are particularly misguided, not 'as well' but 'instead'.

We say they are misguided because in a literate society the primary identification of anybody, or any body, must be verbal: a name, printed or spoken. It is not impossible to make a symbol stand for a name, but it can happen only when the symbol has been seen constantly, for many years, in association with the name, so that the association becomes a conditioned reflex in people's minds. This sort of prolonged, continuous exposure is enormously costly. It is perhaps a condition of successful substitution that the symbol should appear not *only* in publicity material but on common goods or widespread premises, like the Johnnie Walker figure on bottles, or the eagle on branches of Barclays Bank. Neither is possible for accountants.

This point should be in everybody's mind when their thoughts turn to symbols. For if a symbol is only meaningful when seen beside the name, it is surely pertinent to ask what function it is performing; for clearly it is not an identifier.

It may, nevertheless, be functional; but since to get a symbol designed may cost many thousands of pounds, it is well to be clear about what the intended function is, and whether it is worth the money.

A symbol may justify its existence if it *adds* something to the image of its owner. A squirrel is an appropriate symbol for the National Provident Institute: it has connotations of thrift. Bovis's humming bird suggests delicacy and precision: 'We are not like other construction companies'. De la Rue uses a medallion portrait of the first De la Rue: 'We are old-established'. A representational symbol gives considerable scope for conveying some aspect of the image you wish to project.

A less demanding, but perfectly legitimate, function for a symbol is to help to distinguish one advertiser from another: not to *identify*, but to give a distinct *identity* (or individuality). Hadfield Paints used a fox to good effect in this way. This does, of course, demand that the symbol used should be distinctive.

Many symbols are simply pictures of the name, where the name is an object, a creature or a character. This practice goes back a very long way in history, to pre-literate times, when trade names were chosen *because* they lent themselves to pictorial representation.

Figure 2 All these symbols have had hundreds of thousands of pounds of publicity behind them. They belong to well-known and successful companies. How many can you put names to?

Phoenix Assurance is a typical example; modern ones include Skipper Sardines.

It is harder to justify deliberately setting out on this course today. Since the picture simply duplicates the name, it is difficult to make it add anything, either by way of image or distinctiveness, unless you can make it very characterful—as, indeed, Skipper's skipper is. Barclays Unicorn, the unit trust group, changed from an heraldic unicorn to a realistic one with this thought in mind. Indeed, there are few things with less individual character than an heraldic beast, unless it is a coat of arms. To the casual glance, which is all that such things ever get, one coat of arms is indistinguishable from another. Its sole function is to convey a vaguely 'establishment' image.

The initial trap

Among the things with even less distinctiveness than heraldic animals are many of the sets of initials used by businesses to distinguish themselves. To use a firm's initials for this purpose seems, at first sight, like a good idea. They are, after all, much closer to the name than some pictorial symbols, and should therefore be much more readily identified.

The fact is, however, that unless your name is very familiar indeed, people will *not* connect it with your initials. They are bombarded with altogether too many sets of initials as it is, and yours are much more marginal to their lives than most. BP and ICI can get away with it: they have spent millions of pounds on establishing their initials. Within limited special-interest groups, too, it may be possible to use initials on their own successfully: everyone in the City knows what BET stands for. Similarly, everyone in accountancy knows what PW stands for, but Price Waterhouse are wise enough not to try to use their initials on their own, even when talking to the profession.

The only safe rule is that initials on their own do *not* identify. They may, nevertheless, have a contribution to make: if well designed they can make a statement about your personality, your 'image'. The proviso, 'if well designed', is vital; intrinsically initials are very blank and bland, and require original thinking and sensitive handling if they are to convey the impression you intend. Unfortunately good design is rare and expensive, and it has to be said that few of the sets of initials one sees in the papers add anything whatever to the identity of their owners.

A further caveat is that if you use your initials as a symbol they should be recognisably your initials (they are, after all, presumably the way you want to be referred to familiarly). Some designers go to great pains to render the letters they are working on as little like the basic characters as possible, turning them into abstract patterns in which only close familiarity can discern the identity of the advertiser. A favourite trick is to embellish them with arrows

Figure 3 It seems fair to ask what designs like these add to the identity of the companies using them.

pointing this way and that and intended, no doubt, to convey ideas of aspiration or ubiquity. Like most cliches, they actually convey nothing at all. People have better things to do than work out this sort of private symbolism.

Using initials as part of your identity demands as much thought, and no less design ability, than using a pictorial symbol. If they do not identify and add nothing by way of distinctiveness or character, you are better off without them.

Initials and abstract designs are sometimes distinguished from representational, pictorial symbols by the term 'hard-edge', as against 'soft-edge', the 'soft-edge' symbol being the pictorial.

The logotype: a picture, not a word

The way you display your name in print, whether it appears on its own or in association with some kind of graphic device, is called a 'logotype'. It is important to remember that, unless it is in a very simple, classic typeface, a logotype works more like a picture than a word. The more it has in the way of design values, the more it will function—in communication terms—like a picture.

If you have this kind of logotype (or 'logo' as it is generally called), you cannot use it in a headline. It will disrupt the communication. *Figure 4* shows the effect.

A logo of this kind should be used only at the foot of an advertisement, as a sign off, or on the cover of a booklet as a kind of seal. It will not work as part of a sentence.

More to it than your name

It is not only by your name, and the way you display it, that people will recognise you in print. If you take copies of *The Times*, the *Daily Telegraph* and the *Observer*, and fold them so that their banners are obscured, you will have no difficulty in telling one from another. Their whole typographical look is distinctive.

So the differences between typefaces that we drew attention to when discussing name styles are important in all parts of printed communication. In planning how to present your corporate personality you will need to devote great care in choosing a typeface that you can use *everywhere*.

Your chosen typeface must of course reflect the character you wish to project; and it must be easy to read. These are the two overriding needs. Do not strive too hard for other qualities: distinctive-

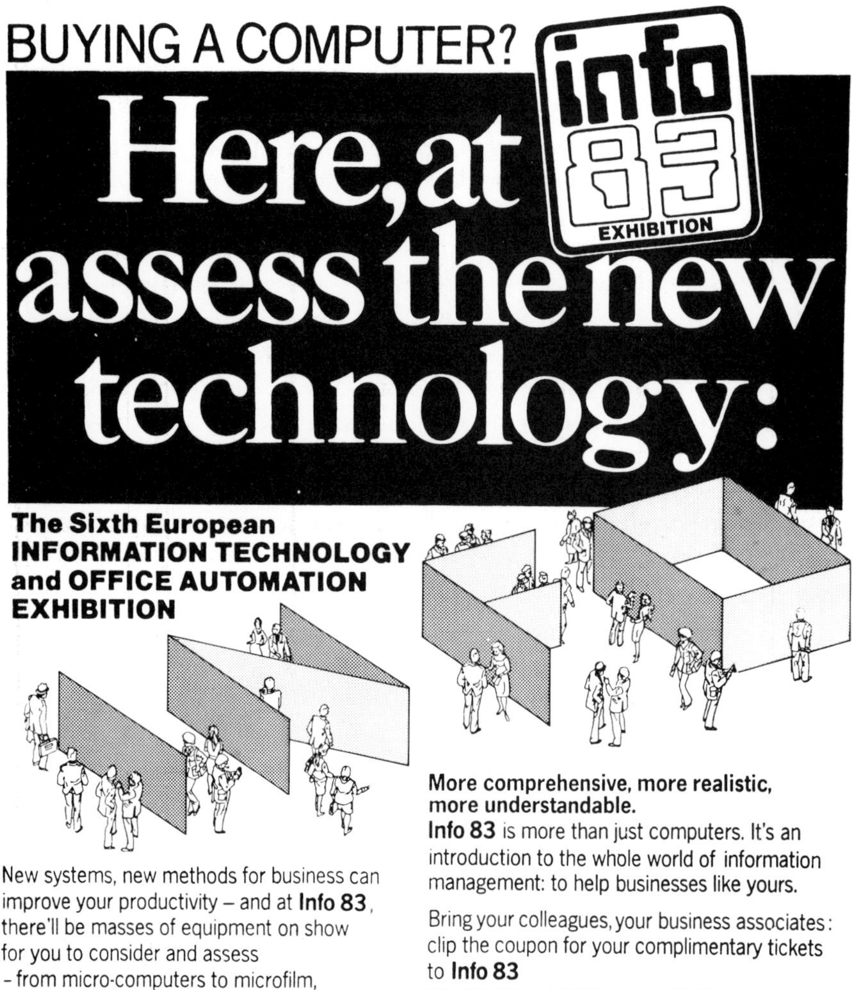

Figure 4 A logotype is a picture, not a word, and does not work as part of a sentence.

ness can be a snare. A 'distinctive' type is all too likely to look self-conscious, and may also look old-fashioned after a few years. Very soon it will embarrass you.

There is nothing against using one type for headlines (and your logo) and another for the body text. You may, for example, feel that a 'sans-serif' type (see *Figure 5*) exactly expresses the image you want. Use it by all means for headlines, but be very wary of using it for text. Serifs (see *Figure 5* again) give sparkle to a page of type and make it look more inviting to read. They are also an aid to the eye in distinguishing letters and words. Sans-serif type, on the other hand, tends to look grey and uninviting in the mass.

There is an idea, sometimes encountered among non-practitioners, that sans-serif type is somehow more modern and 'efficient'. This view was briefly prevalent among professional designers about sixty years ago, but its short-comings were soon realised; nothing that impairs communication is efficient. You will not see sans-serif type used in newspaper stories, though you will often see it in headlines. Newspapers are the supreme professionals in communication.

Typeface is not the end of it, either

There is more to the look of a piece of print than the typeface in which it is set. The size of the type, both absolute and relative, is also

Serif Sans Serif

Serif Sans Serif

Serif Sans Serif

Figure 5 Serif type, on the left, has short transverse strokes at the terminals of characters. Sans-serif (right) dispenses with these.

important. So is the amount of white space, and how it is disposed. So is the question of whether you should have a border or rule round your advertisements, and if so of what kind. So too is the matter of photographs versus drawings, if you are contemplating illustrations.

There is merit also in the idea of having a 'house' colour, to be used on all print. All these things add up to what is called your 'house style', and in laying down your house-style you can specify as many of them as you think appropriate. To specify typeface or faces is, we suggest, essential. A minimum type *size*, for the sake of legibility, is also useful. For the rest, you will have to weigh the desirability of uniformity against the need to retain some flexibility.

The choice between photographs and drawings, for example, depends very much on what you are trying to do in any particular instance. For verisimilitude, for conveying conviction that this is how it really is, you need photographs. More generalised visual statements can be made with drawings, which also have the advantage that they generally have a more distinctive style than photographs. A corollary of this is that cheap drawings can do more harm to your image than cheap photographs.

Be consistent

Having decided on your house-style, use it consistently, and use it everywhere. Use it on stationery, as well as advertisements and booklets. Your letter-head is the vehicle for your most frequent contact with your clients, and arguably the most important of all. If your new name-style has been worth devising, it is worth using everywhere. Do not go on using the old letter-head just because you have some in stock.

It may be, of course, that you will decide that the name-style used in your existing letter-head is exactly what you need, or that there is so much goodwill in it that you cannot afford to change it. This is a perfectly valid decision, but make sure the name on your letter-head has the necessary weight and authority to hold up in the newspapers.

Make sure, too, that the letters that go out under your name are all typed in the same way, with the same margins, the same line spacing, the same rule as to indentation of paragraphs, the same position for the signature and the recipient's name and address. Little touches like this all help to convey the impression of a firm that knows exactly what it is doing.

Make sure that everyone concerned with communication with the outside world knows what your house-style is, and sticks to it.

Do you need a slogan?

One more possible feature of your public personality remains to be touched on, since it is widely believed to be an essential ingredient of advertising. That is the slogan.

A slogan is a terse and (its inventors hope) memorable summation of some aspect of a firm's service, product or personality that is felt to be particularly important. It is a *summation*, and is therefore not the same as a headline, whose function is to induce readership by holding out a promise of some kind. It can sometimes stand on its own, but generally comes at the end of a selling argument: if in a press advertisement, next to the logotype. Usually, but not always, it is intended to have a long life, and some have lasted for decades, like 'Players please', and 'Don't be vague, ask for Haig'.

Many successful advertisers do without slogans, and adopting one is a course strewn with pitfalls. It is all too easy to appear slick or brash, or to give the impression that, like the coiners of political slogans, you are trying to pre-empt thought. Since advertising for service industries is generally intended to elicit a thoughtful response, this can be counterproductive, to say the least.

The wrong way to approach the question of a slogan—and a very common one—is to decide that you've got to have a slogan, and then, from those submitted, choose the one that nobody actually dislikes. You are likely to end up with something that will have become an embarrassing incubus after two or three years.

The right way is to go back to your marketing strategy to decide exactly which aspect of your image is the absolutely essential one, and encapsulate that in three or four words—*without trying to be clever*. The ideal slogan short list has only one item on it.

Not only, therefore, are you not obliged to have a slogan if you advertise. It is better to do without one until you are sure you have got it right.

Chapter 5

THE USES OF ADVERTISING

How advertising works

You advertise because you want members of a particular group—your target audience—to use certain services that you offer, but this straightforward—indeed obvious—statement covers much that is far from straightforward and not always by any means obvious.

Very little advertising works, or is intended to work, by persuading people to commit themselves then and there. The nearest it comes to this is usually in mail-order advertising, which is intended to get people to send off an order, usually with money, straight away. It does this by saying, in great detail, exactly what the deal is. Even so it can work only with people who are actually *in the market* for that particular thing at the moment they read the advertisement. One of the arts of mail-order selling lies in choosing articles for which enough people will be in the market at the moment the advertisement appears.

One of the things you know for certain about your audience is that only a tiny proportion is actually *in the market* at any time—in the sense that they are so dissatisfied with the service they are getting that they actively want to change; or have never had that particular service before and are actively seeking it. Moreover, it is most unlikely that you will be able to say enough, within the confines of a press advertisement, to describe what you are offering in sufficient detail, and if you could, there is too much at stake for a prospective client to commit himself 'off the page'.

The best *immediate* result you can hope for is that they will want to know more about you; that they will send for more details—which is why you must have a booklet—or, best of all, pick up the telephone. Even this is unlikely to happen before they have seen your advertisement several times. Conventional wisdom—which may in this case be correct—says that an advertisement has not done its job until it has appeared six times. People have to be under a very compelling need before they will respond to the first sight of an advertisement.

(One consequence of this is that you should not stop running an advertisement too soon. The point at which you start to become bored with it is the point at which people out there start noticing it.)

It seems likely that advertising is powerless against entrenched attitudes and convictions. It cannot push water uphill or persuade anybody that black is white, but if there is the tiniest crack in the dyke of complacency, well-directed advertising can enlarge it until a new realisation bursts in. A scintilla of dissatisfaction with things as they are must exist before advertising can implant the notion that they might be better.

This does not imply 'knocking'. The phrase 'dissatisfaction with things as they are' embraces situations in which the prospect becomes aware of a gap in the range of services he is receiving. Even if you hope to take advantage of dissatisfaction with someone else's service, there is no need to knock, even by implication. Positive statements about the benefits of your service are quite enough—probably *more* effective, indeed.

Possibly, if the advertising is particularly relevant and compelling, some memory of it is stored up and released by some appropriate trigger at a time when action is called for. Possibly it works by bringing awareness of the product or service closer to the conscious level, so that when the need arises, yours is the first name the prospect's mind fishes out.

'It seems likely . . .' 'Possibly . . .' It will not have escaped you that we are doing no more than advancing hypotheses. The truth is that nobody knows for certain the precise mechanisms by which advertising works. The only hard fact seems to be that it does.

One persuasive theory has it that advertising does not work directly at all; that the only thing that persuades people to buy is the personal recommendation of their friends, and that advertising works by reassuring people who are already customers that they have made the right choice; then they pass on their satisfaction to their friends. Some proponents of this idea claim that it even applies to off-the-page selling: that people do not buy in this way unless they know someone who has. In favour of it is the undoubted fact that once you have bought anything, you immediately start to see advertisements for it. They were there all the time, but you didn't notice them.

Selling your services v selling yourself

Granted that the effect of advertising is slow and cumulative, that it cannot reach more than a very small number of 'ripe' prospects, and that *awareness* is what really counts, why advertise services at all? Why not concentrate on getting your image *as a firm* to the top of people's consciousness?

This is one of the strands of thinking that leads to what is called corporate advertising. Another school of thought argues that corporate advertising is a waste of money. Their argument is that practically nobody is ever in the market for accountancy services in general. They do not say to themselves 'We need an accountant'. They say 'We need such-and-such done. We must find an accountant to do it.' The need for an accountant arises from the perceived need for a specific service. Moreover—so this argument continues—the face you present to the public *is* your services. You are not knowable through any other medium.

Both arguments are persuasive—so persuasive indeed as to point to the possibility that both are correct, and that it is possible to reconcile them. So it is.

The core of the counter argument is that people will read only about things that interest them, and, unless they are actually in the market for your services, they are not interested in what a super lot you are. Proponents of corporate advertising have to take this fact aboard. Corporate advertising must relate whatever it is you want to say to something of interest to the people you want to say it to.

Fortunately the list of such things is very long. It could be nothing more than entertainment—much successful corporate advertising is entertaining. It could be an issue of general concern, like the environment, unemployment, the depletion of resources, inflation, productivity or people's standard of living. It could—even in this country—be patriotism, if you can find the right balance between flag-wagging and the usual embarrassed mumble.

It must, however, be something to which you can *genuinely* link some aspect of your firm and its activities, its character or achievements. A strained or bogus link will excite derision and work against you.

Remember, too, that different audiences are interested in different things, and that the things of which you are particularly proud may interest a very small audience indeed—perhaps just the readers of one particular supplement in one particular publication. Before you criticise someone else's corporate advertising, think to whom it is addressed. It may be just the shareholders, or the company's suppliers, or even Parliament and the Civil Service. All such groups are legitimate targets for corporate advertising, the objective of which is to create a favourable climate of opinion among any group that may influence your business success. It is in its corporate aspect that advertising comes closest to public relations.

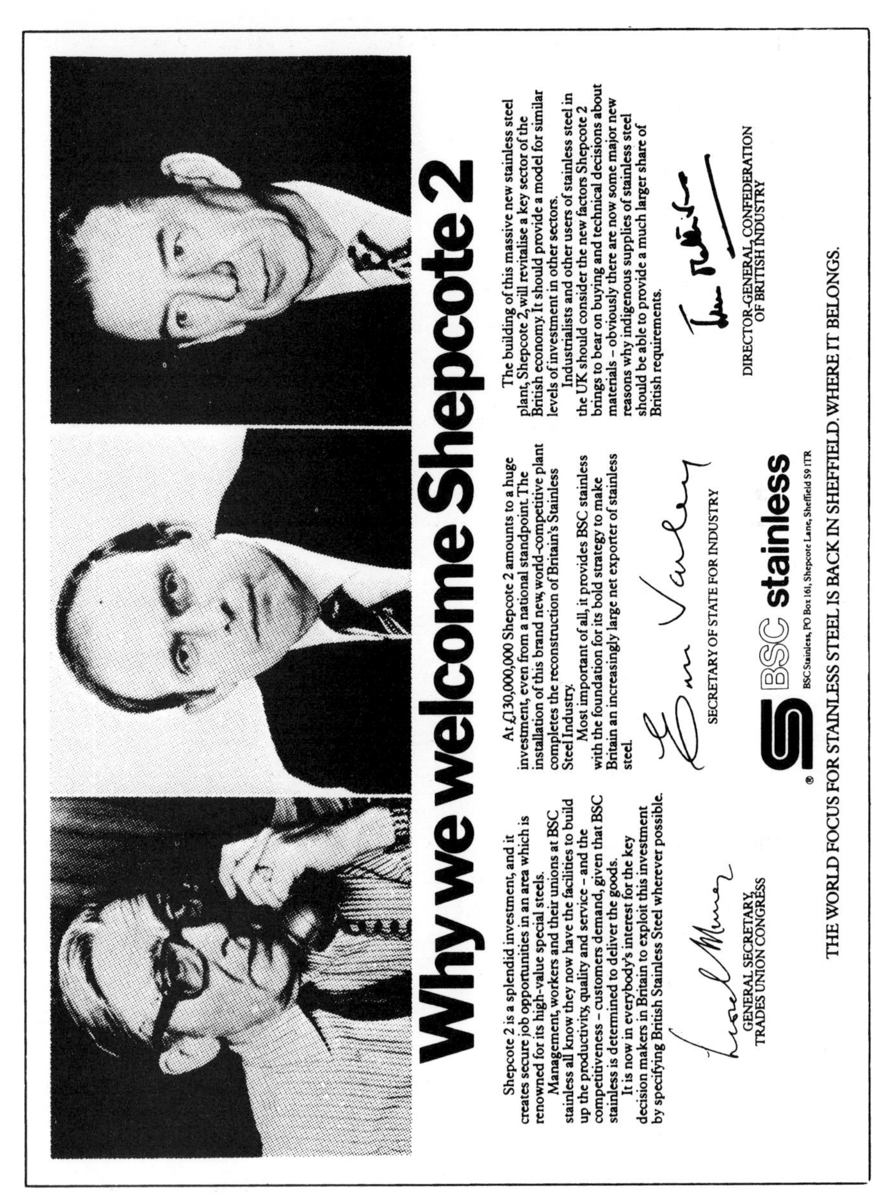

Figure 6 Excellent corporate advertising, touching on people's concern about unemployment and Britain's international competitiveness, and exploiting readers' interest in what three well-known faces have to say.

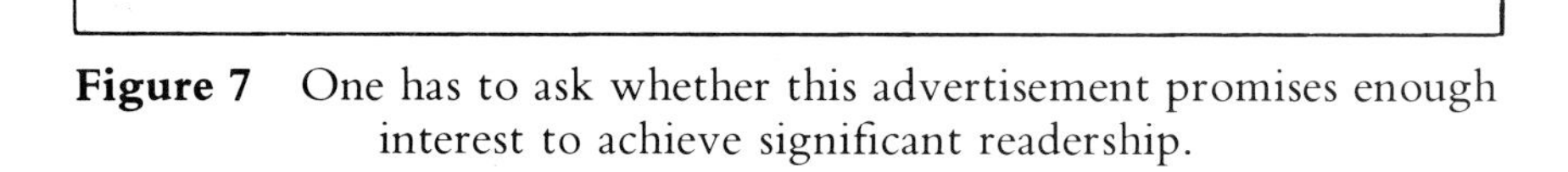

Figure 7 One has to ask whether this advertisement promises enough interest to achieve significant readership.

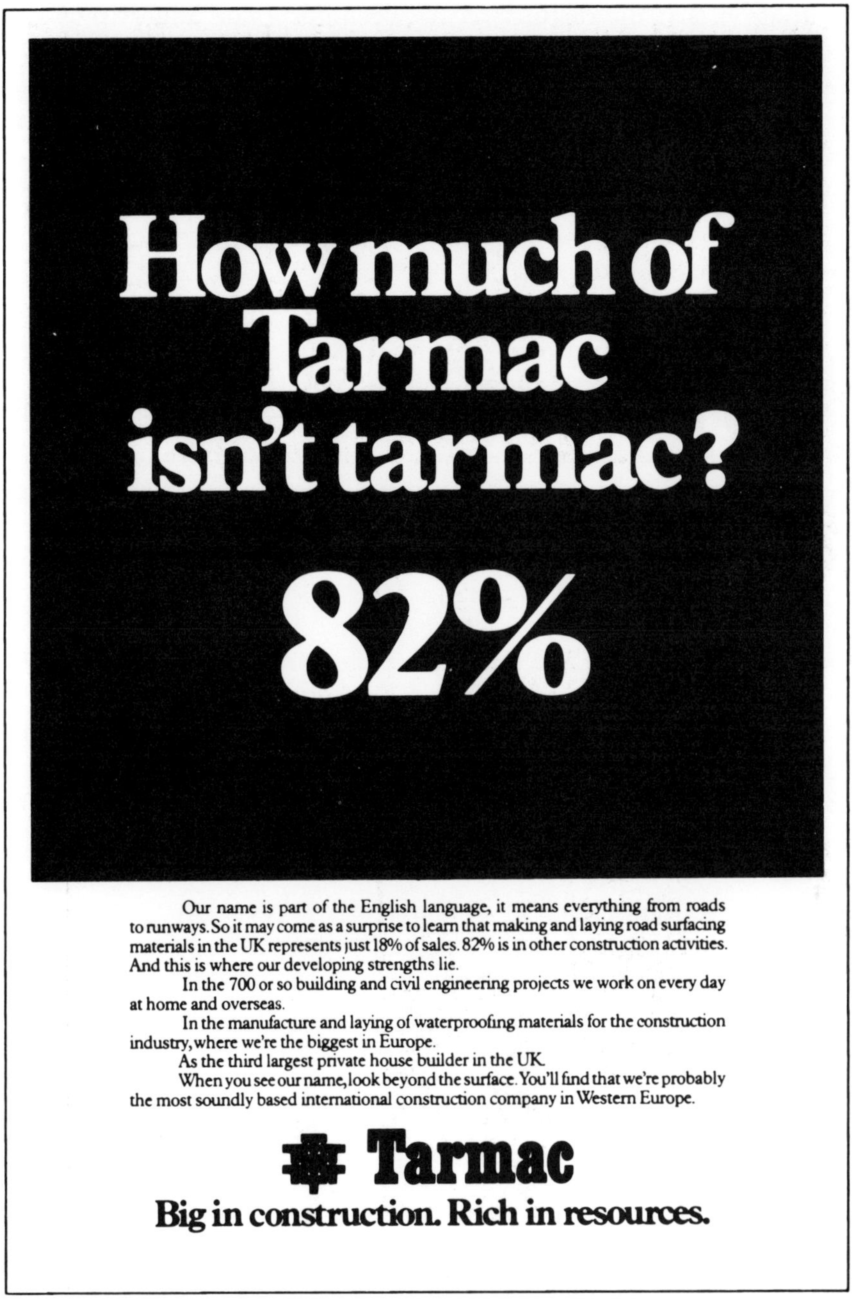

How much of Tarmac isn't tarmac?

82%

Our name is part of the English language, it means everything from roads to runways. So it may come as a surprise to learn that making and laying road surfacing materials in the UK represents just 18% of sales. 82% is in other construction activities. And this is where our developing strengths lie.

In the 700 or so building and civil engineering projects we work on every day at home and overseas.

In the manufacture and laying of waterproofing materials for the construction industry, where we're the biggest in Europe.

As the third largest private house builder in the UK.

When you see our name, look beyond the surface. You'll find that we're probably the most soundly based international construction company in Western Europe.

Tarmac

Big in construction. Rich in resources.

Figure 8 Correcting a misunderstanding—an advertisement of interest only to the City of London, but a good and legitimate use of the medium.

Perhaps the ultimate reconciliation of the two views is the realisation that the distinction between corporate advertising and 'selling' advertising is, in fact, an unreal one. All advertising is corporate advertising, because there is no way in which it can avoid conveying some impression of the advertiser *as a firm*. All corporate advertising must offer the reader *something*, because otherwise nobody is interested. People are highly resistant to propaganda.

The interest of topicality

One thing that is always interesting is News. It is often possible to find, or manufacture, *occasions* for advertising.

Some of these are presented to you in the normal course of things. There is a Budget at least once a year, sometimes more often, and if you specialise in tax, any budget is an occasion for advertising. Almost any taxation change can furnish an excuse for you to tell people about your service, and because it is topical it will stand a very good chance of being read.

Topicality is a well-tried readership technique. Legislation bearing on company law could provide an opportunity for you to demonstrate your expertise and your speed of reaction. A change in institute rules is another occasion of the kind that you could turn to your advantage.

Moving to new premises, or opening a new office, are legitimate occasions for an announcement. It is a pity, however, to waste it with a *bare* announcement. Build in some 'sell', and make the most of it. If you are involved in a merger or take-over, that too is news and an occasion to be exploited for publicity.

Specific things you can offer do not have to be limited to your services. If one of your partners writes a technical manual, its publication is a publicity opening for the firm. You could indeed consider making a regular thing of this, and publishing under your own imprint. Then you will get more of any kudos there may be, and begin to establish yourself as an authority.

If you are able to produce a commentary on matters of topical interest, this could also be offered in an advertisement; similarly with research reports on, for example, the impact of specific taxes, or inflation accounting. The object would be, not so much to sell copies, but to establish the name of your firm as an authority on a particular subject.

Recruitment: the changing scene

In the years before the liberalisation of the rules governing advertising, recruitment advertising, it has to be admitted, was sometimes undertaken more for the sake of the advertising than for the recruitment. This is not to say that genuine vacancies did not exist: it would have been unthinkable to attract applications for jobs that were not there. But when a firm had no other way of getting its name before the public, it was natural that it should place advertising to fill vacancies without enquiring too closely whether advertising was in fact the best way to fill them.

Other pressures could produce the same result. When someone leaves a firm, recruiting a replacement may seem urgent. There is a temptation to pick up a telephone and place an advertisement without delay. It may not be the right response.

A careful analysis of your manpower needs could lead to the conclusion that it is not really necessary to replace the leaver at all. Why did the person leave? Perhaps he had not enough work to keep him happy. If a replacement is really essential, do you have to look for him outside the firm? Internal promotion is cheaper and better for morale.

In short, recruitment advertising, like any other kind, demands careful pre-planning in the context of a long-term strategy. If this identifies a need for additional qualified people, then well-aimed, well-constructed advertisements are an efficient way of finding them—and will continue to be a valuable means of presenting yourself to the business world. Incompetent advertising, on the other hand, not only produces a flood of unsuitable applicants (especially in a recession), but gives a poor impression of the firm.

An unquestionable, continuing need—at least for the larger practices—is to maintain a flow of new entrants to the profession. It could be argued that this is a job for the Institute, not individual firms. In practice it is very doubtful whether advertising for recruits to accountancy in general would have the bite or impact of numerous firms all competing for good people. It might provide useful background, but it is the actual employers that generate response.

The success of the university milk-round really depends on the ground being prepared beforehand by advertising. The appropriate advertising for this purpose is, of course, quite different from advertising to fill specific jobs. It is *career* advertising, addressed to people who have only hazy ideas about what an accountant actually does. *Job* advertising is addressed to the qualified, and quite different considerations apply. Both must adhere to your laid-down positioning.

Recruitment advertising and related PR activities are dealt with at greater length and in more detail in other chapters. (See pages 63 and 77 respectively.)

Chapter 6

WHERE TO ADVERTISE

Your strategic planning, and the early stages of your tactical planning, should have defined the people you want to influence—your *target audience*. In the final stage of tactical planning it is necessary to define very precisely the means by which you intend to reach them—your *media*, in fact (a word that signifies no more than 'means').

Drawing up a media plan is a highly complex business, often involving a computer. To do it cost-effectively is a job for professionals. All we aim to do in this chapter is to give you some idea of the considerations that guide the professionals, and the terms they use, so as to help you understand their recommendations.

What is available?

The available media in this country are newspapers and magazines, the trade and professional press, television, radio, outdoor and direct mail. Each has different characteristics, in terms of whom they reach, their cost, and what you can do with them.

Newspapers and magazines include some of the media likely to be of most interest to you. The *national newspapers* are published in London, but many of them have regional editions. *Provincial dailies* are published in the main commercial centres outside London, though most of them have London offices and London editors. The main provincial centres also have *evening papers* (there is no national evening paper; the *Standard* covers only the Home Counties). *Local papers* serve much smaller areas: part of a county, or the catchment area of a market town; they are all weekly or bi-weekly.

Not everybody, even in the target audiences in which you might be interested, reads a national newspaper. Provincial dailies have, in the areas they serve, equivalent standing, and are the sole daily reading of many businessmen. Local newspapers enable you to be very selective in terms of the area you reach, but their penetration of the business community is patchy (penetration is a measure of the extent to which a paper is read by any particular target audience).

The very wide readership of the nationals means that, inevitably, you pay for a great many readers who are of no interest to you; but sometimes this can be acceptable.

The Trade and Professional Press is much more selective than any newspaper in terms of the occupation and interests of its readers. There is much less wasted circulation. For that reason it is relatively more expensive—its cost-per-thousand (readers) is higher. Most specialist fields are covered by more than one journal, and to use all of them can bring the absolute cost up to a level at which the cost advantage against the nationals looks much less attractive. For example, a page in each of the three main accountancy journals would come to 70% of the cost of comparable space in the *Financial Times*.

All printed media share certain characteristics. They are highly flexible as to the size of space you can buy, and hence what you need to spend. They allow you to develop your argument at any length you think necessary, and they allow the reader to go back over what you have said, to re-read it or put it aside for future reference.

None of this applies to television or radio.

Television is the mass medium par excellence. It allows a certain amount of selectivity in the area to be covered, but not very much in the composition of the audience—though the time of transmission affects the latter, and can be exploited. For example, particular groups can be reached by transmitting during programmes of special interest to them. In this field some interesting developments are on the way: Channel 4 is planning a financial programme, and Cable TV opens up the possibility of very much more specialised programming.

Television is the most expensive medium in absolute terms; and the cost of producing a television commercial is many times higher than for a press advertisement.

As a general rule, television time is sold only in 15 second modules: you can buy 15, 30 or 45 seconds, or a minute, but not as a rule 10 or 20 seconds. It is not possible to say very much in 30 seconds (the commonest length of 'spot'); and, of course, viewers have no opportunity to check on what you have said.

Radio has similar characteristics. It is, however, very much cheaper, both in air-time and production costs and it allows rather more geographical flexibility: radio stations cover smaller areas than television stations.

Do not dismiss the electronic media out of hand. In some circumstances, and for some purposes, they can be cost-effective.

American accountancy firms have used television. The IBA rules governing financial advertising have recently changed, and there may be a trend towards companies using television to announce or comment on their company results. The medium can also be used effectively to generate demand for booklets: viewers are given a telephone number which they can use to order copies. Holiday firms demonstrate every year that this technique works.

Outdoor advertising includes posters of all kinds, tube cards and bus-sides (collectively known as transport advertising) and panels in taxis. Taxi-panels are obviously seen mainly by the well-to-do, but other outdoor media can be selective only in a geographical sense: it is possible to choose poster sites so that posters appear only in business areas, for example (where, however, sites are often in short supply), or near your own offices, perhaps in order to show people how to find them.

What you can say on a poster is, if anything, even more limited than what you can say on television. There is one exception: posters in stations on the London Underground can carry long copy, since people read them eagerly while waiting for trains. In general, though, they work best as reminders of something people have seen elsewhere.

Direct Mail, if intelligently carried out, can be a very efficient form of advertising, but is not at present permitted by the Institute.

How a media plan is arrived at

A media plan starts with a target audience and *either* a budget *or* a communication target; this may be expressed as the number of 'opportunities to see' (OTS) that you wish each member of the audience to have, or as the coverage you want to aim for (the percentage of audience you wish to reach)—or both. Generally the budget is fixed in advance, and the planners try to achieve the best coverage and OTS they can within the limits it sets.

Another constant that may be built into the media plan from the start is the minimum size of the space (for the press) or the length of spot (for television and radio). Alternatively you can wait for the media planner to tell you what you can afford in terms of size or length. The former is more satisfactory: size of space is not only a function of what you can afford; it also affects the impression you give of yourself, and is governed partly by what you want to say.

The space costs of newspaper advertising are directly related to the number of readers, the number of times the advertisement appears, and its size. Consequently every media plan is a compromise between coverage, frequency and size. For a given budget, the bigger the advertisement, the fewer times it can appear. The more papers it appears in, the less you have to spend on size and frequency. (For the sake of simplicity we restrict ourselves to the newspapers in this discussion. *Mutatis mutandis*, the same applies to all media.) There are other variables as well: you pay more for a 'solus' position (where your advertisement is alone on the page), and more still for a front-page solus. The leader page usually carries a premium, and you pay more for the front half of the paper.

Of the three main variables, coverage presents the most complex problem. This is because:

(a) no single publication covers the whole of any target group,
(b) very few members of any target group read only one paper.

The consequences are best explained by an example. You might find that 60% of the businessmen you are particularly interested in read the *Financial Times*, and 40% read the *Daily Telegraph*; but of those 40%, half read the *Financial Times* as well. So adding the *Telegraph* to your list of papers adds only 20% to your coverage. Adding, say, *The Times* might add only another 5%. The remaining 15% will prove increasingly elusive and expensive, as each added paper adds fewer and fewer readers.

This is where a computer can be useful. It can calculate the combination of papers, and the number of insertions in each, that will give you maximum coverage at minimum cost.

The figures on which the computer operates are provided by an enormous mass of data produced by *media research*. The research is done either by independent organisations like JICNRR (Joint Industry Committee on Newspaper Readership Research) and JICTAR (Joint Industry Committee on Television Audience Research), or by the newspapers and television companies themselves; the latter's figures obviously need careful scrutiny. Broadly speaking, the object is to find out who reads what.

For such data to be of any use, people have to be classified; otherwise no numerical values can be allotted to 'who'. The basic classification, in use for a generation or more and still of value, is by socio-economic groups: A, B, C1, C2, D and E. For most purposes you will be interested in A and B, though you may recruit from C1 (clerical lower-middle class).

But this is a fairly blunt instrument, and much more refined classifications are now available. It is possible to find out what papers are read by businessmen in general; by finance directors; by accountants; by directors of manufacturing companies, engineering companies, nationalised industries and many others.

Press Advertising Schedule - Proposed

Publication/Circulation	Size/Position	No. of Ins.	Cost Per Insertion	Total
Financial Times	21cm x 3 cols Ft.Page Solus	4	3,300	£13,200
	21cm x 3 cols Ft. Page Solus	2	3,650 est.cost	7,300
	13cm x 2 cols Yr.Savings & Invs.	5	858	4,290
Daily Telegraph	13cm x 2 cols City	10	1,248	12,480
Sunday Telegraph	13cm x 2 cols City	10	910	9,100
The Times	13cm x 2 cols Business News	10	390	3,900
				£37,070
Reserve for additional advtg (based on results of July/ Aug. campaign) say:-				
The Observer	12cm x 2 cols Observer Bus.	4	672	2,688
The Guardian	13cm x 2 cols City	4	312	1,248
Sunday Times	13cm x 2 cols Business News	4	1,601.60	6,406.40
				£47,412.40
+ 0.1% ASFB surcharge				
All rates subject to confirmation at time of booking.				

Figure 9 A typical media schedule, the working document for

Period: Sept '84 - July '85

Date: 9th July, 1984.

Sept.	Oct.	Nov.	Dec.	Jan.	Feb.	March	Apr.	May	June	July	Aug.
8	27	17	1								
						16				13	
				X	X		X	X	X		
X	X	X	X	X	X	X	X	X	X		
X	X	X	X	X	X	X	X	X	X		
X	X	X	X	X	X	X	X	X	X		
2 insertions pre-Christmas						2 insertions 1985					

those responsible for getting your advertisement into the papers.

The end result of the media planner's efforts is a 'media schedule', which sets out the plan in detail, in tabular form. It lists the papers, the size of space, the date of appearance and the cost, and may also show the coverage and opportunities-to-see achieved. An example of a media schedule is shown as *Figure 9*.

Chapter 7

WHAT MAKES EFFECTIVE ADVERTISING?

You will probably not, in general, be writing booklets or advertisement copy yourself, but you will be called on to evaluate what other people have written, and for anyone new to it this can be perplexing. You may know that you do not like it, but that is not enough. In the first place, saying 'I don't like it' is not the way to get something better. In the second place, whether you like it or not is not in fact the first question that should be asked—though it is a perfectly fair one, to which due weight should be given. The first question to be asked is 'Will it work?'.

This chapter is intended to give you some objective yardsticks by which to judge advertising copy and design. You should also find it helpful if you are ever called on to do any writing yourself.

Before an advertisement or booklet (or, indeed, an ordinary business letter) can do any persuading it has to overcome three hurdles: it has to be noticed; it has to be read; and it has to be understood.

There are many ways of making sure you are noticed, but one overshadows all the others. It is to make sure that what you say is *relevant* to the intended reader.

The Principle of Relevance

You will sometimes hear it said that there are no rules in advertisement. We feel bound to say that this is sloppy-minded. It is believed by people who do not care to submit to mental discipline or to accept that, in advertising, technique is more important than inspiration. There are rules, and the first and greatest of them is the Principal of Relevance. Indeed, it has almost the status of natural law, like Newton's *Principia* or the Laws of Thermodynamics; and it can be expressed thus:

> The attention given to any piece of communication is directly proportional to its relevance to the intended audience.

It is as simple as that: no relevance, no attention. Your advertisement (or whatever) will simply not be noticed, let alone read or acted on.

It cannot be said too often that advertising is *marginal* to people's lives. In the newspapers this marginal thing has to compete with matters that are *central* to readers' lives and interests: other people's follies or misfortunes, babies, beautiful women, royalty, cuddly animals, the gardening column, the wickedness of the government, the price of their shares.

It follows that your advertisement must not only *be* relevant. It must *declare its relevance*, and declare it loud and clear. It has a fraction of a split second in which to grab each reader's attention, and in that blink of an eyelid it has to say 'This is for you'.

The advertisement reproduced as *Figure 10* is addressed to much the same business audience as you would have in mind for yours, but why should they—or indeed anyone else—bother to read it? What is there in it to detain their eye as it flicks over the page?

Defining the relevance

How one expresses relevance so that it is both clear and compelling is mainly a matter of technique. How one arrives at it involves something more—something best defined as *imaginative sympathy*.

Imaginative sympathy is more important than literary skill; more important, even, than the ability to produce brilliant 'ideas'. It is, indeed, the source of good ideas. It preserves writers from the error of writing to please the boss or the client (who is you), and from the vice of writing to please themselves. Above all, it preserves them from irrelevance. If you keep your reader constantly before your mind you will write good copy.

A copywriter must imagine, sympathetically, what his readers' needs are; what benefits and satisfactions they look for in your service; what are the limits of their experience; what they will understand by the sentence he has just written.

At the simplest level one can say that a product or service has certain attributes, and its intended users have certain needs. At some point the attributes and the needs intersect; and at that point you have an advertisement. The intersection defines the relevance.

Of course it is seldom, if ever, as simple as that. Your service has a whole bundle of attributes, and your prospects are not a monolithic entity but any number of individual human beings with different needs. Some of these are felt very deeply, others hardly at all.

To try to hit all needs, at all levels, is to invite failure by being

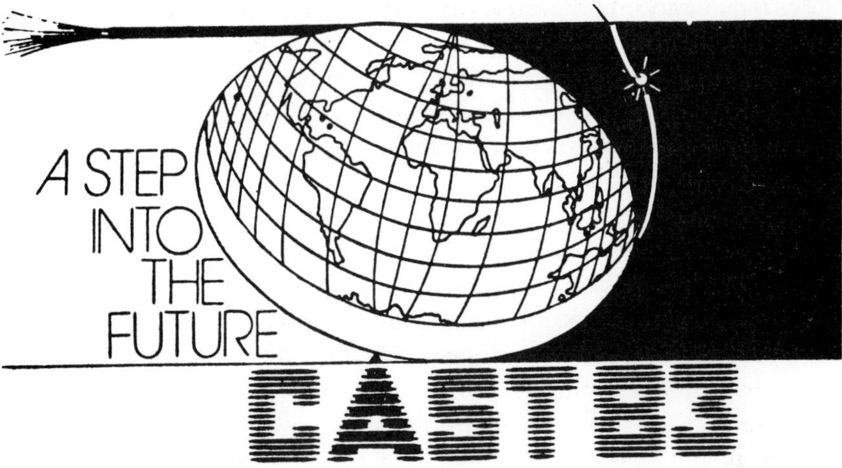

Figure 10 Lack of any obvious relevance makes it unlikely that the intended audience ever noticed this advertisement, let alone read it.

diffuse and, inevitably, confusing. Shooting people know that 'blazing into the brown' seldom brings down a bird. It is necessary to concentrate your communication effort, and say one thing at a time. You cannot really hope to lodge more than one idea at a time in a reader's mind.

How do you decide which attribute to match to which need? You look, of course, for a widely felt need—ideally one felt by almost everybody in your chosen target group. You also look for an attribute that your service has in greater degree than your competitors—ideally a unique one. It must be a real attribute; it must be possible to point to some feature of your service and say, 'Look. This is what brings the benefit we are talking about.' Anyone, however, who finds a unique attribute that meets a universally felt need is an improbably lucky copywriter.

If you're not improbably lucky

It is much more likely that the strongest point of your service is more or less closely matched by at least one competitor. If that is the situation, there are a number of things you can do.

(1) You can introduce an improvement. This can not only give you a marketing advantage but it can also give you a very good basis for your advertisement: NEWS.

(2) You can look for some other widely felt need, which the competition does not at present offer to satisfy. Your imaginative sympathy may suggest what this is; but you may think it prudent to validate your intuition by research.

(3) You look at your service again, and ask yourself if it has some other strong point that can be presented as answering the original need (or some other need that research or intuition comes up with).

It may well be that a competitor—or, indeed, the entire competition—could claim this attribute too. So long as they are not claiming it, this should not deter you. Pre-empt that feature for your own. Competitors will not laugh at you. They will gnash their teeth for not having thought of it first.

A good and straightforward example comes from the field of fast-moving packaged goods. Years ago Macleans Toothpaste ran a campaign based on what they called the Tongue Test. It rested on the observable fact that if you run your tongue over your teeth after cleaning them they feel smooth. Any toothpaste has this effect. Macleans pre-empted it for themselves, and linked it to a particular feature of the product that does in truth contribute to the effect—the fact that it contains a 'lipoid solvent'. Sales responded quite well.

(4) You look for a deeper need. This can be the most fruitful course of all.

If you think hard and honestly about your own motives, you will probably agree that most of your purchasing decisions are made to satisfy needs on at least two levels—perhaps more. You choose a car because it is thrifty on petrol, but also because you feel it is the right car for the sort of person you are.

A car is, of course, pre-eminently and very obviously an extension of your personality, but the same is true of more mundane purchases, and even in the choice of business equipment and services. A businessman makes such a choice not only—perhaps not even mainly—because it will produce the commercial results he wants, but because he sees that choice as being the one that will reflect credit on himself, or because it is consistent with his idea of himself—his character or reputation. We suggest that *every* purchasing decision is to some extent a declaration—usually entirely unconscious—of the kind of person the purchaser thinks he is, or would like to be, or would like other people to think he is.

By digging down to this deeper level of satisfaction you are very likely to find the competitive difference you need, and a relevance the competition can not match. Perhaps they *could* have matched it, but they did not, and now it is yours.

It is extremely important to remember that these deeper, emotional needs are very seldom acknowledged. You can only hint at them—by the situation you adumbrate, by oblique allusions, by tone of voice. To bring them out into the open, explicitly, may embarrass your readers. A scent, or men's fashions, may be sold openly on a self-image platform. Your services cannot. Your prospects *must* be presented with rational arguments at the explicit level. One of their emotional needs is to be able to persuade themselves—and their superiors and peers—that they have acted on the most strictly rational business grounds.

Attitudes

This discussion of people's deeper needs has brought out the importance of their attitude to themselves. Attitudes to the external world are also important in determining how people behave in the market place. The way they see life in general, and their job in particular; their perceptions of other people, and especially accountants; attitudes to tradition, to responsibility, to authority—all these are going to affect the way in which they meet their needs. They may determine whether a particular need is acknowledged, or even whether it is met at all.

Attitudes, like needs, differ in the intensity with which they are held. Some are deeply entrenched, some may be modified quite easily. They are important factors to bear in mind when trying to define the relevance of what you have to offer. They can profoundly affect the way in which relevance is perceived.

Benefits and features

We have now defined three levels of communication. At the deepest level we have the satisfaction of an emotional, non-rational (but not necessarily irrational) need. We have the *benefit* that enables us to offer that satisfaction, and we have the objective *feature* of the product or service that enables us to claim that benefit.

It may well be that the explicit, overt part of the communication may stop at the 'benefit' stage. Stating the benefit may point so unmistakably to the deeper satisfaction that there is no need to nudge the reader in the ribs about it. Every claim of a benefit must be supported by a *fact*, and the fact must depend on a feature.

Benefits and features are not the same. People are not primarily interested in features. They are interested in the benefits that the features bring. Features interest them only as supporting evidence for the benefits you are claiming. The design of the cylinder head may be a feature of your car, but what you are interested in is the extra mileage that results from more efficient combustion. That is the benefit.

Similarly, your intimate knowledge of the tax system, and your understanding of exactly what the local inspector will and will not allow, may be *features* of your taxation service. The *benefit*, however, is the tax saving that results from these; and that is what people are interested in.

Always sell benefits—not features.

The role of research

We have already touched on research as a means of validating beliefs about client needs and attitudes. These beliefs may arise from one's own knowledge of the market, and sympathetic understanding of people, but it is important to recognise that such beliefs may really be no more than hypotheses.

Hypotheses may also be derived from a pilot research—generally what is called 'qualitative' research, in the form of a group discussion, or a small series of unstructured interviews.

It is possible that qualitative research may throw up such clear signposts that it is felt unnecessary to proceed to the more expensive stage of 'quantitative' research. This would be a much larger-scale survey intended to give numerical values to the needs and attitudes suggested by the qualitative work—or for that matter by your intuitions—but if large sums of money are involved it could be unwise not to test ideas in some way. It costs money, but not so much as a failed advertising campaign.

Research will not produce advertisements for you. It can only point you in a direction where the theme for an advertisement or a campaign is to be found. You still need imagination in order to be able to see what the research means in terms of how to match the service to the need, and how to communicate the benefit.

Enemies of relevance

Of all the things that work against relevance, the most pervasive and insidious is cleverness. Writers and artists who are more concerned to demonstrate how clever they are than to communicate a benefit produce advertisements that are an expensive waste of their clients' money.

Look at *Figure 11*. What are we supposed to get out of this? 'Performing zeal' is presumably a pun on 'performing seal'. But having worked this out, are we any further forward? Does anyone want a performing seal—even one that stands on its head? Will anyone recognise standing on one's head as a metaphor for anything they ever do themselves. Relevance has flown out of the window on a gale of self-congratulatory chuckles.

We are not decrying cleverness as such—only the self-indulgent kind of cleverness that obscures relevance. Well-directed cleverness will always produce better, more striking advertisements, that spark the imagination of the reader. The cleverest thing a writer can do is to *say what the deal is*, as simply and clearly as possible.

Another ubiquitous enemy of relevance is an advertiser's justifiable pride in his product or service. It results in advertising

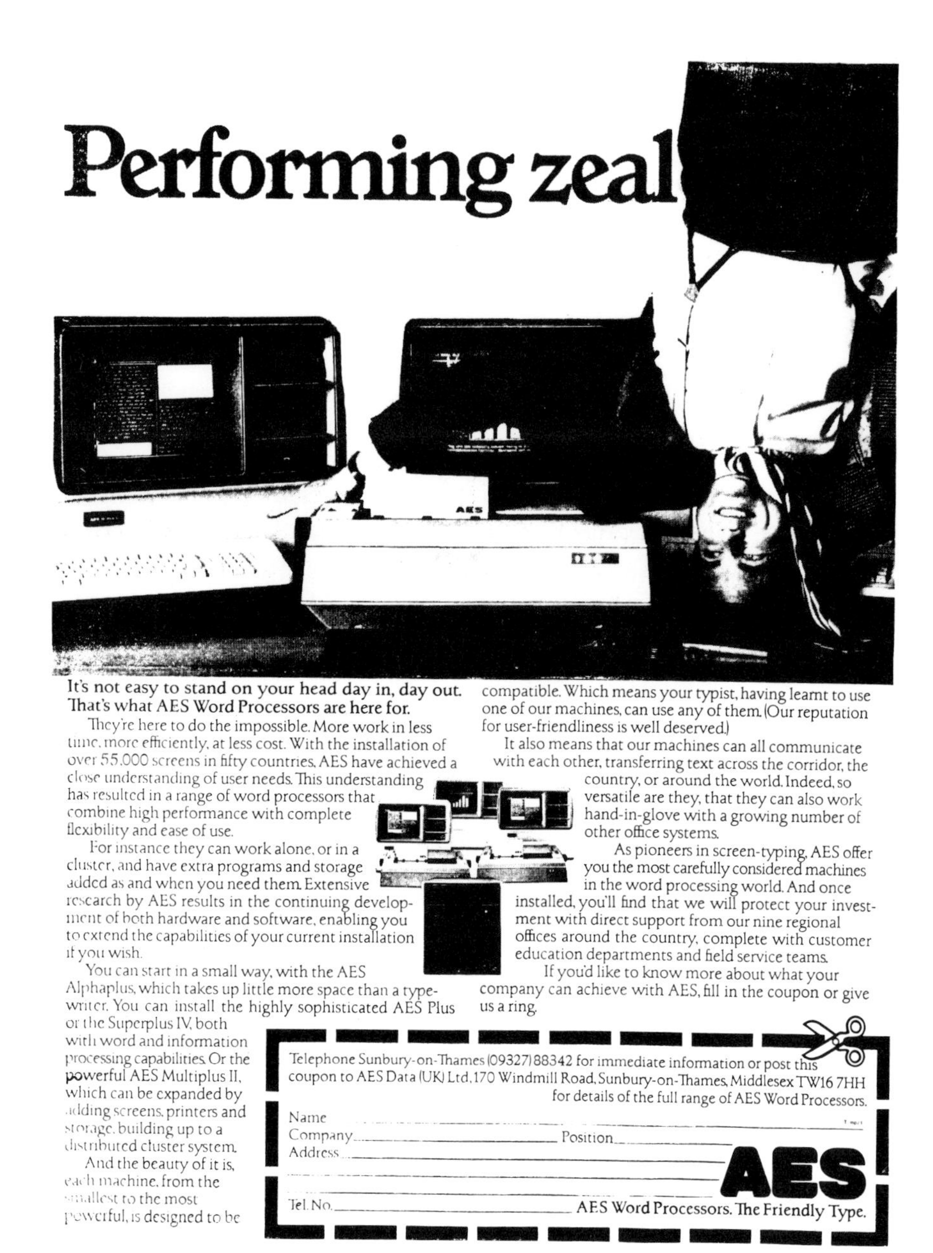

Figure 11 Verbal ingenuity has been allowed to obscure the message.

that is advertiser-oriented instead of reader-oriented; feature-oriented instead of benefit-oriented.

Putting it all together

An advertisement or booklet is not functionally complete unless you can tick every item in the following checklist. The mnemonic by which you can remember it is AID CA.

A—Attention
I —Interest
D—Desire
C—Conviction
A—Action

If you omit the C (giving AIDA) it is perhaps easier to remember, but Conviction is altogether too important an element in advertising to be left out of account. Lack of the 'Desire' or 'Action' elements, or both, is a sure sign that what you have in front of you is not advertising but propaganda.

Let us take them in turn.

Attention Relevance is what matters most when you want attention. Size of space, blackness and boldness of type, drama in the picture—all these can help, but they go for nothing if there is no relevance.

You can get attention of a sort with a picture of one of the Page 3 girls from *The Sun* but it will not do you any good, even if permissible. You need to get attention and *keep* it—at least long enough for your name to be noticed. A Page 3 girl takes attention *away* from your name.

The right kind of attention is gained by a *promise*—the promise of a benefit, or the promise that by reading on the reader will find a benefit.

Interest Interest is what *keeps* attention. (None of these elements is self-contained or independent of the others.) It depends on specific, concrete, relevant *facts*, supporting a claim to a benefit. Human interest may also come in here. Nothing is more interesting than other people. If you can tell a story about how other people have benefited, that is the best kind of fact with which to get and keep your reader's interest.

Desire Promising a relevant benefit should make readers want what you offer. Always look at things from the reader's standpoint, not your own, and not your firm's. What is it that he or she wants?

As desire grows, price begins to become relevant.

Conviction Your entire effort fails if readers do not believe what you say. Much ineffective advertising owes its ineffectiveness to a belief on the part of the advertiser—or his agency—that it is sufficient to *tell people things*. It is not. You have to tell people things *in such a way that the things are believed.*

Partly this is a matter of not over-claiming. One detects sometimes a self-defeating note of hysteria, as though a strident claim were more likely to be believed, but mainly it comes down to *facts*.

Belief in a claim depends on the supporting feature or fact being clearly presented. Facts are believable and are on the whole believed. Facts make the difference between a promise and a boast. Advertising is not the same as boasting. Boasts undermine conviction.

It is all too common to find people claiming that they have 'an enviable reputation'. If they really have an enviable reputation, there must somewhere be evidence to support such a claim. The fact that they do not produce it can only serve to make readers suspect (quite correctly) that none exists. It is painful when people try to cover their nakedness with generalisations—especially such threadbare clichés as this.

It is often necessary to be very selective about the facts you parade. You seldom have space or time to say everything. Choosing the really convincing supporting fact is one of the basic skills of copywriting.

An advertisement is not to be judged by the writer's success in cramming in everything the advertiser wants to put into it, but by his success in giving the reader what he wants to get *out* of it.

Action An advertisement should lead to action, and there should be no doubt about *what* action. Many advertisements are intended to lead the reader to buy on his or her next visit to the shops, or even to order 'off the page', but when large sums are involved, the sale is generally a two-stage or even three-stage process. The advertisement is intended only to lead the reader to the next stage. This may be to send for a booklet, to ask a representative to call, to telephone and ask for more details, to have a demonstration or a free trial.

Your advertising will be in the latter category. The advertisement is intended to initiate a process that, if it is to result in a commitment, must culminate in a face-to-face meeting—probably more than one. The first action could be to send for a booklet, or to

"When my husband said he'd leave me everything, I'm sure he didn't mean all this."

Imagine that your husband suddenly died. (It's unthinkable we know. But you really should think about it.)

The very next day an Income Tax demand might drop onto your doormat. Would you know whether to pay it or query it?

You might find yourself with a substantial sum of money from a life assurance policy. Would you know how best to invest it?

Overnight, your husband's business might become your business. How would you cope with being a managing director all of a sudden?

They're tricky questions at the best of times.

But when you've just lost your husband? Well, they could be the last straw.

They don't have to be.

That's because at Lloyds Bank we're in a special position to offer assistance.

We can, for example, assist in the running of any business interests.

We can administer your husband's estate, handle your life assurance claims and adjust your own Will to provide for the children.

We can help fend off the Inland Revenue. And we'll even assist you with your future investments.

It will be useful to have a little money easily available in a savings account but you'll probably want to get the rest earning you a steady income.

In that case you might consider the Lloyds Extra Interest Account. At the moment, it pays 8¾% interest with just one month's notice of withdrawal.

But perhaps more importantly, it pays that interest monthly – a godsend if you've just lost your other regular source of income.

If you would like us to send you our specially prepared brochure please send off the coupon.

Alternatively, your local Lloyds Bank manager and his staff will be happy to give you any information you might need.

In fact they'll lay the foundation of a sound financial future, leaving you free to rebuild something much more important. Your life.

Post to: Russell Smith, Dept T.S. Lloyds Bank Plc, 71 Lombard Street, London EC3P 3BS.

Please send me a copy of your brochure on wills, executorships, estate planning and related services.

Name_____

Address_____

DTS

I am/am not a customer of Lloyds Bank.
(Delete as appropriate)

Lloyds Bank

Rate correct at time of going to press, but may fluctuate.

Figure 12 A well-constructed advertisement, with all the parts working together to make a clear and persuasive whole.

telephone for information—which in turn should lead to an appointment.

It is obviously important that the desired action should be made as easy as possible. This is why one sees coupons in advertisements. Do not be misled by the superstition that important people do not fill in coupons. They may not do it themselves, but they get their secretaries to do it. Some years ago the Central Office of Information ran a campaign to encourage companies to set up in the Development Areas, where a number of financial incentives were offered. The advertisements were all couponed, and the coupons were used. Many replies were received that did *not* use the coupon; but would there have been as many if there had been no coupon there? One of the functions of a coupon is simply to signal, by its presence, the kind of action that is called for.

The carpentry of print

Producing advertisements is not a form of art, whatever the pretensions of some of its practitioners. It is a craft. Its products, unlike a work of art, have to fulfil a pre-determined purpose, and are to be judged by their success in fulfilling it.

At its best, an advertisement may be a Chippendale chair, produced by a craftsman who has much of the artist in him. It should never be less successful than the effort of a journeyman joiner, humbly making a serviceable stool. We do not judge either to be a good piece of furniture if it does not support anyone who sits on it.

Whether it is a successful advertisement depends not only on the relevance being right, but also on the skill with which its elements are put together. For lack of this, some advertising falls to pieces.

Printed communication may consist of any or all of the following elements:

1 Display words
2 Pictures or other graphics
3 Captions
4 Text

1 DISPLAY WORDS are those set in a type strong enough to stand out from other matter, or to stand on its own. Such are headlines (or titles, in booklets), subheads, cross-heads, slogans and names. Sometimes captions are so bold as to be display.

Normally, display is reserved for words that *must* be taken in at first glance, or before other elements, or before the eye leaves the advertisement or booklet altogether. Consequently it should be used sparingly: 'when everybody's somebody, then no one's anybody'.

Headline or title The function of the headline or title is to declare the relevance of what follows. It may share this function with a picture or some other graphic device (diagram, chart, map, etc).

There is a grammatical relationship between headline and picture; it may be analogous to the relationship of subject and predicate in a sentence; or it may be expressed in the unspoken words 'like this'.

There is also a functional relationship. If the headline comments on or explains the picture, it will function partly as a caption to the picture. One looks for captions underneath pictures, and if a headline is intended to function as a caption, underneath the picture is where it ought to be. Conversely, if it is under the picture but does *not* have the attributes of a caption, the reader will be confused. He will try to interpret it as a caption and be baffled because it does not conform to his expectations.

There is also a functional relationship between headline and text: the headline should make the reader want to tackle the text. It should have what's called 'come-on'.

A headline accompanied by a picture should, therefore, face both ways: into the text and into the picture.

Subheads amplify headlines. The headline and subhead format can be very useful if, in order to declare the relevance adequately, you need more words than can be set in type of a dominant size. A short headline in large type, with an amplifying subhead in smaller type can solve the problem. But each part must be self-contained. The effect of a marked change in type size is analogous to a full stop.

Cross-heads have two functions, psychological and logical. Psychologically, they encourage the reader to persevere, by breaking up large areas of type, and signalling, 'Look, here's something interesting!'. Their logical function is to establish priorities and connections: which parts are logically subordinate to others, and which are linked in 'sets' of equal logical status. To reflect a graded logical hierarchy, it is essential to have a graded typographical hierarchy.

In this passage, 'Headlines', 'Subheads' and 'Cross-heads' are all of equal status, but are logically subordinate to 'Display Words', which in turn is logically subordinate to 'The Carpentry of Print'.

Long text should always be broken up by cross-heads.

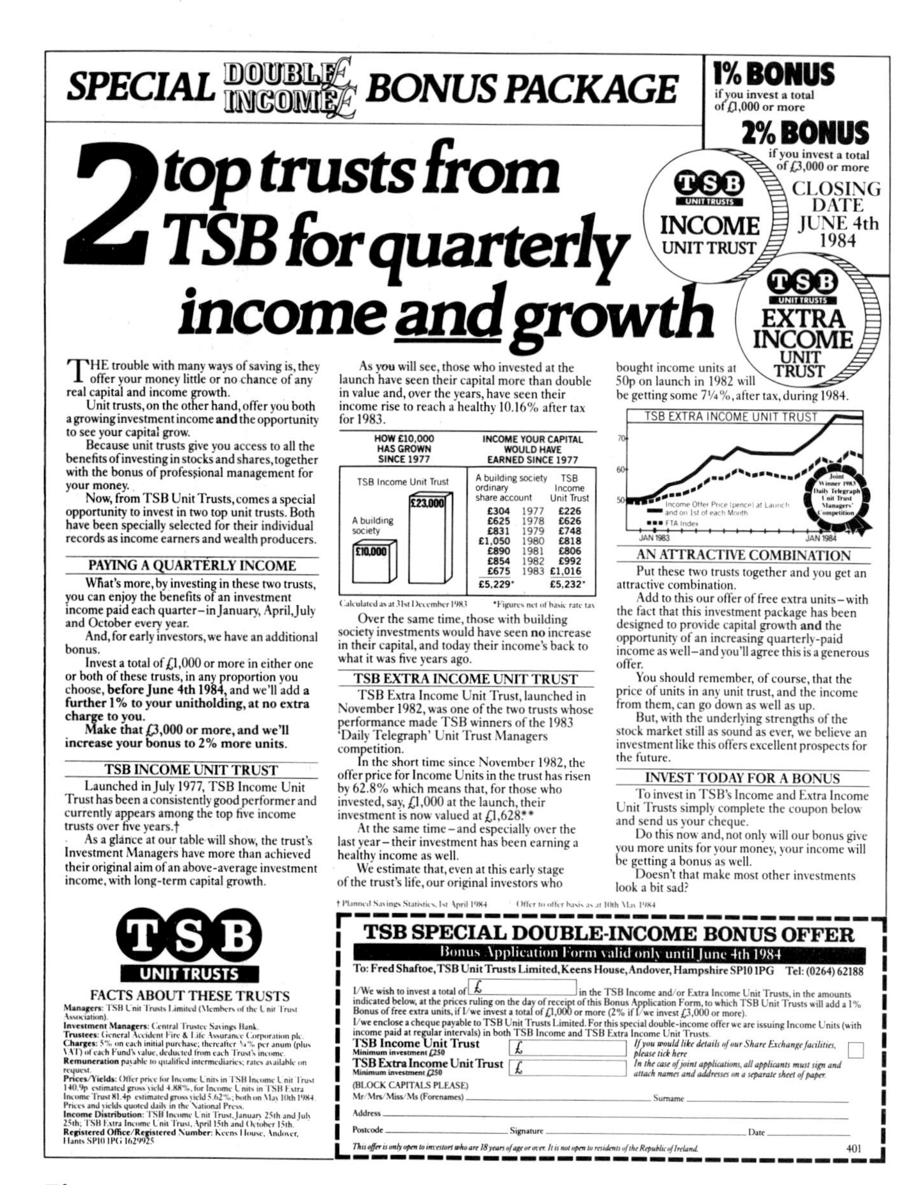

Figure 13 All the elements work together coherently in this well constructed advertisement.

Cross-heads that do no more than announce the category of subject next to be dealt with (eg 'Introduction', 'Our Services') are very much less effective in encouraging the reader than phrases offering a benefit or promising interest or a challenge (eg 'The right size for your accountants', 'How we can improve your profitability').

Slogans encapsulate a selling message or an aspect of a company's image. They sum up what has gone before. Consequently, they work very badly when forced into the role of headlines.

Names The true function of a displayed name (other than in the headline) is to 'sign' the communication—to put the advertiser's stamp on it and establish its legitimacy and authority. Establishing what is being advertised is not a burden that should be laid on it. A good advertisement does this with its bottom right-hand corner covered up.

Remember that if you want to attract someone's attention it is better to whisper his name than to shout your own.

2 PICTURES A picture may be a self-contained unit of communication, so explicit that it can stand on its own. Normally, however, it will need a caption.

A picture should always *add something* to the total communication. Its content or mood should convey something that the headline or title cannot say, or—for the sake of effect—chooses not to say. It will not do this if it is simply a visual rendering of a verbal metaphor used in the headline.

Compare *Figures 14* and *15*. In one, headline and picture work together, each complementing the other, cogently, wittily and aptly. The other is a feeble visual rendering of the headline, adding nothing—except perhaps a certain repulsion.

3 CAPTIONS A caption explains or comments on a picture. This close functional relationship should be reflected in a close spatial relationship: the caption should be on or under the picture. If you have several pictures and several captions, it will help to avoid confusion if each caption stands in the same relation to its picture as every other.

4 TEXT Text can never stand alone. It needs display words to give it context and relevance, and to attract attention to it.

Text is built up of sentences arranged in paragraphs. The sentence is now such an elastic organism that grammarians have almost given

Figure 14 An excellent example of the headline-picture relationship. Neither works without the other.

At last there's a word processor that won't stretch your arms, break your nails, or make you go cross-eyed.

It's the new ICL Word Processor. Unlike most word processors, it's not just a glorified typewriter for the odd letter or document, it's a hard-working nine-to-five computer system, to take a load of work, and worry, off your shoulders.

And since it's designed with heavy usage in mind, it's designed to special high standards to minimise fatigue and maximise comfort, qualities glossed over by most word processor manufacturers.

It's simple, very attractive, and beautifully easy to use.

And, most important of all, it can produce first class reports, documents, letters and even has a built-in calculator package.

And because ICL is Europe's leading computer company, with thousands of satisfied users in over 80 countries worldwide, we can offer a quality of business applications experience and ICL Trader Point service back-up that's second to none.

The ICL Word Processor also represents an exciting new springboard for you. The beginning of an Office System Network, in which co-related ICL products will meet all your needs. And that may not be so far in the future as you think.

So take the first step now. Fill in the coupon.

Adjustable screen angle to minimise eyestrain

Big 15 inch screen with easy-to-read gold on bronze display type

Lightweight keyboard for convenient positioning

ICL Word Processor

trader point

To: ICL Trader Point, ICL House, Putney, London SW15 1SW.

Name

Position

Company Name & Address

Telephone

Type of Business

Figure 15 A picture that adds nothing to the headline; it does not help us to imagine the applicability of the headline to our own circumstances, since it carries the metaphor no further.

up the attempt to define it. Try 'A meaningful group of words that is grammatically independent'. Nothing there about verbs, or subjects or predicates. If you try anything like that you quickly find valid exceptions.

Short sentences are easier to handle and easier to understand. Both writer and reader can too easily lose their way in long ones. One authority gives 17 words as the maximum length. We feel this is too arbitrary, and that a better rule is to limit yourself to no more than one subordinate clause. Do not try to put over more than one idea at a time in a single sentence. Vary the length of your sentences. If they are all the same length the effect is monotonous.

Paragraphs, properly used, have an important function. Each stage in a narrative or argument should be given a separate paragraph. Paragraphing will then help the reader to find the way, by signalling the end of one stage and the beginning of the next.

Paragraphing also breaks up the text into digestible-looking pieces. But the fad of treating each sentence as a paragraph throws away a very useful communication tool.

Text should be as short as it can be and as long as it needs to be. There is no maximum length for text. Conversely, text can nearly always be cut, but there comes a point at which it is possible to cut only by resorting to generalisations. This can be fatal to readership.

Use generalisations as little as possible. *Generalisations are boring.* Specific *facts* are what make copy interesting. They will often make it longer, but never generalise to save words. People will not read boring copy, however short it is. They *will* read interesting copy, however long it is.

We have in front of us two magnificently produced booklets published by two internationally respected accountancy firms. One has quite short text, consisting almost exclusively of abstractions and generalisations. The effect is both boring and boastful. The other is full of concrete examples of how they have helped clients (all anonymous). It is readable and convincing.

Both firms make a point of the care with which they recruit people. But where one is content with the generalisation, the other has a diagram showing the number of applications, the number of interviews and the number of actual appointments. Facts clothe the claim in believability.

Above all, try not to *start* with generalisations. You will lose half your readers before you are fairly started. This is what lies behind the often-quoted advice to take infinite pains over your first paragraph, because you will then find that the rest comes easily. Then, when you have finished the piece, go back and cross out your first paragraph. You will often find it was just so much cranking up.

The way the text is laid out has important effect on its readability. Breaking it up into paragraphs makes it *look* more inviting. So does a generous provision of cross-heads. The length of each line is also critical. There is a relationship between the size of type being used and the length of the line of type. The smaller the type, the shorter the line it will stand. If the lines are too long, the eye tends to lose its way as it flicks back to the left-hand edge of the column, and reading becomes difficult. Another way of saying this is that the width of the columns of type is a point to watch. Newspapers use narrow columns, it is worth noting.

Common pitfalls

To describe all the traps that await the unwary writer would fill a book—even if one restricted oneself to the things that really matter, which concern clarity, not 'correctness' or elegance.

One of the points that really matters is so common, however, and matters so much that it deserves a brief mention. It is the failure to make clear how far the force of any grammatical/logical connection is meant to carry.

A common form taken by this failure shows up as unintended links between words. Sometimes the effect is ludicrous, as in the wartime newspaper headline 'Chinese generals fly back to front'. Or this: 'About 15% of men will delay reporting sick too long. Sergeant Majors usually arrive to report sick feet first.' Sometimes it is mystifying, as in this advertisement headline:

GREAT BRITAIN IS GREAT EXHIBITION

Some device was needed to make it clear that what was meant was an exhibition entitled 'Great Britain is Great'.

Another, seen recently, announces:

For trouble-free
letting go
to XYZ

Because 'letting go' is a phrase in its own right, putting it on a line by itself severs the intended connection, which was 'trouble-free letting'.

You have to puzzle readers for only a fraction of a second, and you have lost some of them.

Another common form taken by this fault is mistreatment of the word 'and'. Many people were taught at school that 'and' should occur only once in a list, and that you should never have a comma in front of it. This is a modern superstition. Consider this, from a computer advertisement:

> 'It will handle invoicing, payroll, bought ledger, simplify ordering and stock control.'

The writer has failed to notice that there are actually two lists in this sentence, each dependent on a different main verb. Consequently the force of the verb 'handle' carries on, confusingly, into the second list, dependent on 'simplify'. It should have read:

> 'It will handle invoicing, payroll and bought ledger, and simplify ordering and stock control.'

A comma is needed after 'ledger', to separate the two lists and limit the force of 'handle'.

A common vice is to abuse the freedom—a glorious feature of English—to use nouns as adjectives. The effect is ambiguity. What qualifies what? How far does the force of the qualification carry? This is one of the things that make computer-speak so impenetrable.

> 'At each stage the system remains completely source and object compatible with earlier option levels.'

> 'DDS, Screen Editor, ITS and Reportmaster improve development and maintenance staff productivity.'

Is 'development' meant to qualify 'staff'? Or is it a noun, the object of 'improve'?

'A refresher course on speaking and presentation technique': does the writer mean 'techniques of both speaking and presentation'? Or are the techniques those of presentation only?

Clarity is all. Spare no effort to be clear and unambiguous, and style will come.

Points to watch in layout

When the eye alights on a piece of printed communication, it tends to go first to that part of it that is visually 'strongest'. It may be the biggest, blackest type; it is likely to be the picture, if there is one; if the picture has a strong emotional charge, it will certainly be the picture.

The tendency is then for the eye to go downwards, because that is what our everyday reading habituates us to, and finally leave the page or advertisement at the bottom right-hand corner. If you want the eye to deviate from its accustomed path you have to provide very clear signposts for it.

This is why the commonest form of layout has the picture at the top, the headline under the picture, the copy under the headline and the advertiser's name in the bottom right-hand corner. That is what *works* best.

If you put the headline above the picture, or the copy above the headline (as in *Figure 16*), there is a grave danger that they will be missed altogether. It is not something that should be done at the whim of a designer, but only if there are compelling communication reasons for it, and only with well-contrived graphic safeguards.

The copy should begin as close to the headline as possible. If a picture interposes, the reader may be momentarily at a loss—and that's all you need to lose him. Attention is a fragile thing, especially attention to advertisements. In *Figure 17*, for example, there is a strong temptation to begin at the top of the middle column.

Another common and amateurish error is to treat the headline as the first sentence of the copy. To understand the body copy you have to carry on the sense of the headline into it. But this is not how people read, as you can see for yourself by considering how you read the newspapers.

In booklets, slightly different considerations apply. The eye's natural tendency is to go the right-hand side of each opening, as it is exposed. It is therefore good practice to use the left-hand page of each opening for a picture. If you want to use it for text, make sure there is a strong visual accent to draw the eye there—a bold headline or an interesting small picture.

In folders, each successive unfolding should reveal the next logical stage in the (metaphorical) unfolding of the story. What is folded under, out of sight, should be parenthetical or illustrative, and not an essential part of the developing argument.

A note on Recruitment Advertising

All that we have said about constructing effective advertisements applies with equal force to recruitment advertising.

The Principle of Relevance, for example, demands that you

Figure 16 The copy-headline-picture format, reversing the conventional arrangement, runs grave dangers—especially when, as here, the headline depends on the copy for comprehension.

"A wise man knows when he is well off."

Aesop

"Prosperity Share."

Bradford & Bingley

Figure 17 The reader is meant to start reading the body copy under the picture on the left. The natural tendency is to start under the headline, at the top of the middle column.

identify the job as accurately as possible in the headline. 'ACCOUNTANT' is a better headline than the name of your firm, however well known. What we said about the way to attract someone's attention applies just as much to recruitment advertising. Better still would be

ACCOUNTANT
Cost and Management

Avoid using your own internal terminology for job descriptions unless you are certain it is widely understood.

The next most important thing is the salary, and this should always appear in the subhead. If a company car is provided, this should also go in the subhead:

'£10,000 + car'

None of the reasons generally advanced for omitting any mention of salary are persuasive. It creates the worst possible impression: either that the salary offered is so low that you are ashamed of it, or that existing employees are underpaid—in which case the new entrant could face resentment. Phrases like 'salary commensurate with age and qualifications' succeed only in suggesting that you have no salary policy at all.

It has been estimated that omitting the salary can cut response by up to 80%. The least you should do is to quote a range.

The only other thing you should consider for the subhead is the location. Even if it is not obviously attractive it can perform a useful function, because it can help to aim the advertisement accurately. It is no good getting applications from Southend for a job in Birkenhead, if the applicant is not prepared to move, while for people near Birkenhead proximity will be an attraction.

Only the most compelling reason justifies omitting the name of your firm; the right place for it is at the bottom, as a sign-off. If you really have to be anonymous, place the advertisement through a consultant. There is abundant evidence that box-numbers cut response. In any case, unless you are *very* well-known, say as much about your firm as you can, but don't make exaggerated claims about your size and standing. They undermine belief.

Describe the job soberly, accurately and specifically. Say what the holder of it actually has to *do*. Use specific, active verbs, not vague ones like 'attend to'. Don't oversell, with words like 'challenging' or 'exciting'. Clichés like this convey no precise meaning, and serve only to deter the intelligent—while doing nothing to deter the dullards.

Avoid phrases like 'the successful candidate'; impersonality is alienating—say 'You'.

'You' has another advantage. It enables you to comply with the Sex Discrimination Act without clumsiness—'he/she'—or such ludicrous locutions as 'draughts-person'. In fact most of the job descriptions you are likely to use are accepted as being genderless: 'accountant', 'manager', 'executive'.

Say *why* the vacancy has arisen. This will make the job more interesting, and prevent any suspicion that you suffer from high staff turnover.

Be cool about fringe-benefits. Occasionally you see perfectly commonplace benefits described with a sort of breathless excitement that can only cause derision. The people you want *expect* pension schemes and four weeks holiday and the rest of it.

State the qualifications and experience necessary, simply and factually; give any age limits. But don't specify the number of years experience, or the age, if in fact you are going to be flexible about this. Be wary of abstract personal qualities like 'leadership', 'drive', 'motivated'. Nobody is going to admit—even to themselves—that they lack them; in any case they convey little hard meaning. 'Proven track record' is no better, besides being a worn-out cliché.

Finally say quite clearly what action you want the reader to take.

Generally your aim is a small number of highly suitable applicants, and this is where skilful drafting comes in. Anyone can summon up a crowd of duds.

If you follow these guidelines you should get the people you want. And a most valuable by-product will be that you will project the *personality* of your firm. This is important not only for its effect on potential recruits: a vital part of your target audience is composed of careers advisers at all levels, and—for the young—parents as well. Even when you are looking for mature recruits, there is often a reader over their shoulders—a wife, or husband, or trusted friend. Never lose sight of them.

It is worth taking some trouble to evaluate response. If you log the results of each advertisement and analyse it by media, size and content, you will build up a most useful bank of knowledge, which you can use to make your advertising more cost-effective. It is worth varying the content of your advertisements in order to see whether one aspect of your firm is more attractive than another.

Finally, if you do not get the results you expect, do not assume that the advertising is the culprit. It may be, but there are many other factors at work. Possibly your interviewers are not up to the job; interviewing is a skilled job, and untrained people can give altogether the wrong impression of your firm. Perhaps your salaries or working conditions have fallen behind the competition. Perhaps the action you suggest at the end is inappropriate or off-putting: having to write for an application form is a sure-fire response cutter. Having to telephone without being given a name to ask for is another. As with all advertising, you have to think yourself into the reader's skin.

Chapter 8

PUBLIC RELATIONS

Immense benefits at little cost

Although the publicity generated by Public Relations appears in newspaper space or air-time for which you do not pay, it should not be thought of as 'free'. There are costs involved, whether you employ a consultant or do it yourself. Considerable planning and effort is involved on somebody's part. There is either an overhead to bear, or a fee to pay.

But properly understood and properly applied, PR can bring immense benefits for very little cost. The effort and expense are many times repaid.

It is not without pitfalls. If misapplied, by someone who does not understand what he is doing, PR techniques can backfire. There ought to be a warning printed on this chapter: 'PR can seriously damage your reputation'. And this is perhaps a good argument for *not* trying to do it yourself.

The object of PR is to shift public opinion in a direction advantageous to you. Its techniques can be applied to everything you do of which the public is aware—or can be made aware. Conversely, everything you do can be evaluated in the light of PR; and in the more marketing-minded organisations, this does indeed happen. The main means by which the public can be made aware of what you do is, of course, the media—press, television and radio. Consequently your relations with the media are of the first importance and are the subject of a special area of expertise called Press Relations.

In fact, Press Relations are so important that some people talk as though Press Relations and Public Relations were the same thing. They are not, and it is important to remember that they are not. Otherwise some of the simplest and most vital aspects of Public Relations may be overlooked.

One such simple and obvious aspect is making sure that your receptionist/telephonist is always polite and helpful. Her voice and manner can be warm and outgoing, conveying a genuine concern for the caller's convenience and interests; or they can convey that she—and, by implication, you—could not care less.

Other PR activities are more complex. Some, indeed, can hardly be undertaken without training. None should be embarked upon without careful preparation. And there is nothing of which this is more true than your relations with the media.

Rewarding contacts

The immeasurable value of favourable mention in the press or on the air is that it is more likely to be read or listened to, and much more likely to be believed, than almost anything in paid-for space. People do not, on the whole, believe that advertisers actually tell lies; but they do expect them to present only the good side of their products or services, and suspect a certain amount of exaggeration. The editorial content of press and television, on the other hand, is generally trusted, with some allowance for known political leanings. 'If it's in the papers there must be something in it,' is a widely held belief, even among those who know that the papers sometimes get things wrong. They may make mistakes, but their impartiality in non-political matters is not suspect.

Most journalists, in fact, are conscientious, and do not like making mistakes. They spend much of their working life cultivating useful contacts—people to whom they can turn for reliable information and authoritative opinions. Here lies your opportunity.

You cannot make the media print or broadcast the things you would like to see and hear. They will use only what they think their readers and viewers will be interested in. Nor can you stop them printing or broadcasting the unpalatable. But you *can* make certain that it is to you that they turn for views on the news, and that, in anything that affects your firm directly, they understand your point of view and your intentions, and have all the relevant facts.

What all journalists have in common is an enquiring mind, but this does not mean that they are digging for dirt. They are not trying to catch you out. You will find them inquisitive, but what they are digging for is *understanding*. Help them to that and they are on your side. They want the background to the news, as well as the news itself. They like to be able to ring round for comment when a story breaks. They want to know who is rising to the top, and what their views are.

It is a Fleet Street saying that a journalist is only as good as his contacts. If you are a useful contact, if your information is helpful and reliable, you will earn the trust and respect of journalists and they will turn to you more and more. When controversial issues surface, it should be your views that the media seek. Good PR can ensure that it is.

Cultivating your contacts

The shape of a journalist's working day means that most of his contacts are made at lunch-time, over a lunch-table in someone else's office. But they do not, of course, simply turn up in someone's boardroom and start asking questions over the gin and tonic. They wait to be invited. And the better ones get a very full diary a long time ahead.

So to make sure that your contacts do actually happen, and do not remain merely an aspiration, it is a good plan to draw up a programme of lunches with key journalists, spanning as much as a year. The whole programme needs to be co-ordinated, so that each journalist meets a partner whose specialisation is of particular interest to him or her. Each occasion should be planned in advance, with careful thought given to the topics to be covered and the views to be expressed.

Do not parade the entire partnership, unless you are a small firm. Three or four people are quite enough for your guest to meet. Then there is a good chance that he will go away remembering names and faces, and who said what, and—with luck—with an idea for a future article. If he is confronted by a crowd he may feel that he is being treated like a cabaret turn.

It is an enormous advantage on such an occasion to be able to speak freely and, thanks to the well-understood convention of 'off-the-record' briefings, you always can. If a journalist is told that something is off-the-record, he inevitably respects it. To do anything else would be folly. But it is only fair to say clearly, *before* you start on the subject, that what you are going to say is off-the-record.

Another useful convention is the non-attributable briefing, which allows you to speak your mind on sensitive topics without fear of embarrassment to yourself or your firm.

Bear in mind that newspapers—national, provincial or local—have quite different priorities and interests from specialist and professional journals. Good Press Relations call for an understanding of what each paper is looking for. The national press is writing for an enormous audience, and has to aim at a lowest common denominator of interest. The provincial press writes for a rather more limited readership, and the local press for one to whom even the liquidation of a village grocery shop may be a matter of keen interest. The professional press journalist knows his readers intimately, and can rely on keen interest in highly specialised subjects, the careers of individuals and the fate of small firms.

The manager of your local radio station is another potential ally and a key contact for you. He can be encouraged to turn to you, not only for programme material, but whenever he needs informal help or advice—a background briefing on matters of current interest for example. Then requests for someone to contribute to a programme will follow. A firm that is prepared to field someone who will give a short talk or submit to an interview will do much to establish its professional presence in the area.

The ultimate coup, perhaps, is to get one of your partners on the air, being interviewed about the Budget. It can be done.

An important part of your groundwork is the appointment of spokesmen—one for each office if you have more than one. Journalists like to know who they can turn to. For you the benefit is that you will avoid speaking with more than one voice, and your switchboard will always know who to put callers through to. But *every* partner should be able to talk to the press in case of unplanned contacts, *and should be trained in doing so*, just as every officer in Northern Ireland is trained in talking to reporters or live on television.

You need no reminding that it is your people that are your greatest asset. One of the prime objects of PR is maximum exposure of your best people. This starts with the cultivation of journalists.

How to handle news

Occasions on which your own firm is the subject of a news story will no doubt be rare. But they will occur, and it is important to make the most of them—which starts with being clear about what constitutes news.

Different papers have different definitions of news, and much depends on the scale of the event. The appointment of a partner to handle a receivership or liquidation is always news at some level; whether national or local depends on the status of the company concerned. Much the same applies to mergers between accountancy firms, moves of partners, internal promotions, moving into a new building or opening another office. New developments in accounting practice, or other technical matters, will normally be of interest only to the accountancy press; but some topics, like inflation accounting, will have wider relevance.

The social consequences of a receivership or liquidation demand that the subject be handled sensitively; but equally there is great prestige to be won if the receiver can pull the company round, or the liquidator sell off parts of it as going concerns. In any case, there is no need to be diffident. Consider having the partner concerned talk to the local TV reporter outside your office, with your name in view.

A caveat on mergers is to remember to tell your clients about them before you tell the press. Reassure them that no change in the people they deal with is contemplated. Tell them all about the benefits. There are legitimate advertising opportunities to be found here, too.

Moving offices or opening a new department is an occasion for a party. Whatever the occasion you are exploiting, think about the PR angle *early*, before other plans have crystallised.

Press Releases are the means by which you communicate news about yourselves to the media (television and radio as well as the press). Writing them is a specialist skill: a good advertising copywriter may write inept press releases—indeed is quite likely to do so, since the last thing an editor wants is 'sell'.

A good press release gives the facts, coolly and without embellishment. It is as short as possible, but gives *all* the relevant facts: let the recipient do the selecting. Deciding what are the relevant facts is part of the skill. Newspaper space is a commodity in very short supply, and all journalists expect to see most of what they write end up 'on the spike'. Keep it crisp and clear, and go straight into the facts, so that it is easy for the paper to see whether it is of interest.

The classic route to a good press release is embodied in the six questions: Who? What? When? Where? How? Why? Possibly not all of them will be relevant, but this makes a very useful check list.

It is perfectly legitimate to add some comment, indicating why the reported event is important to you, and pointing out any long-term implications. This might take the form of a quote from the senior partner. Quotes always make good copy; and it is best to name the source—attributed quotes are more interesting, and more convincing, than the remarks of Mr A Spokesman.

Always end by giving a name, and telephone number, of someone to whom further enquiries can be addressed.

Press Conferences should be reserved for really important events, like mergers between two firms of standing, either locally or nationally. They need very careful organising and handling, and the best advice we can offer is to entrust the job to professionals. They can also brief and rehearse you to ensure that as far as possible you are fully prepared. There is no need to appoint full-time consultants in order to get this done: they will be quite happy to do it on an ad hoc basis for a modest fee.

If the matter is a sensitive one, you can consider imposing an 'embargo', which bars publication before a predetermined date. Journalists invariably respect embargoes.

Generating publicity

So far we have considered mainly what can be done to take advantage of events—outside events in many cases, and, even if initiated by you, not initiated with publicity in mind. This may be called Reactive PR. But there is another kind of PR, which may be called Active PR. It generates activities for the sake of their PR value.

Examples include the running of seminars and courses, the publication of reports and surveys, contributing articles to newspapers and professional journals, and sponsorship of events.

Seminars, courses and conferences, if well conceived and organised, earn the gratitude of participants and enhance the authority of the organisers. But they are very expensive, and a more economical road to the same results is to offer people as speakers at other people's seminars. Most such events are not run by firms in competition with you, but by organisations that make their living that way. An offer to contribute a speaker is very often most welcome.

There is no doubt that a firm that takes the lead in explaining technical change to clients and others (including non-professional audiences) will earn prestige.

If you do run one yourself, it is essential that it should be adequately publicised. Sometimes they are run with a newspaper as co-sponsor. It is also essential that all speakers should be very thoroughly rehearsed, and if necessary coached in public speaking. Confused material and mumbling delivery do more harm than good.

Publications work for you in much the same way. You may already have a programme of publishing technical research—on tax, or liquidations, or statistical sampling techniques, for example, or discussion papers on necessary changes in the law. It is perfectly legitimate that the PR value of such things should be one of the factors you consider when planning it.

If anyone in your firm has special expertise in any particular branch of accountancy, or special experience with any particular branch of industry or commerce, it should be possible to get publicity mileage out of it. There is always an intermittent demand for authoritative articles in the Press—national, local and professional. To satisfy it will put your name before interested sections of the public in a most favourable light. Good relations with the Press are, of course, a useful precondition. They will improve the chance of acceptance, and ensure that you have early warning of any relevant feature or survey.

Involvement with the Institute, and with District Societies, is to be encouraged. Partners might seek election to committees—anyone who attends meetings regularly will sooner or later find themselves asked to join a committee—and could also volunteer to speak at conferences. All these activities can be seen as aspects of Public Relations: the aim is maximum involvement, leading to maximum exposure.

You should also consider joining the CBI, the BIM and your local Chamber of Commerce, if you have not done so already. All can lead to useful contacts; but beyond that they have PR value, projecting an image of an outward-looking firm, with interests beyond its professional field. Taking on the Honorary Treasurership of local charities or voluntary bodies also creates a good impression.

Sponsorship is another aspect of active PR, and sufficiently important to warrant a section of this chapter to itself.

The value of patronage

Patronage—the encouragement and sponsorship of worthwhile activities that have no obvious business connections—has long been a permissible activity for accountants. Relaxation of the rules limiting other activities has not lessened its value.

Sponsorship is perhaps most commonly associated in the public mind with sporting events. Our own opinion is that you should not necessarily dismiss this as incompatible with your professional status. Golf or tennis would be highly appropriate. The people whose participation and interest they attract include a high proportion of the managerial class; and the fact that you may not be able to do it on a national scale should not deter you. A local tournament would attract no less keen interest in your area, and a local club would welcome your support. Sponsored runs could also be considered.

The commitment does of course involve rather more than putting up prize money: many hours of time must be put in. A partner will have to present prizes and make a short speech; staff will have to be committed to organisation and liaison with the clubs. But this is true of any worthwhile PR activity; and good consultants will relieve you of much of the burden.

The preparation calls for great attention to detail. It is surprisingly easy to overlook such matters as ensuring that your name is prominently displayed at the award ceremony—especially if there is a co-sponsor. It has been known for one sponsor to crowd out the other altogether. Press and TV coverage should be arranged.

However, sport is not the only thing you can sponsor. If you wish to present a more thoughtful, 'cultured' image, sponsorship of concerts and art exhibitions can be useful. Their middle-class audience makes them very appropriate. Concerts especially are with difficulty made self-supporting financially, and sponsorship is always welcome by the organisers—who often include influential local people.

Education is another field for sponsorship. Endowing a university chair or postgraduate research is perhaps only for the largest firms. But a series of lectures at the local polytechnic can be set up at lower cost, and a book-keeping prize at a school should be within reach of most practices. To endow a prize marks you as a firm with a concern for high standards, and you do not have to limit your horizons to your own discipline. Related subjects, such as computer science or business studies, are also worth considering, and local schools and colleges should prove co-operative. It is of some interest that Lloyds Bank have sponsored an archaeology award.

The size of the prize is not of the first importance: people enter as much for the honour as for the money. But you will have to devote some effort to it, not only in the judging but in the choice of judges, who must include independent people of at least local distinction.

Sponsorship generates goodwill and excellent publicity. Even if it does nothing but getting your name before the right public it is valuable. But when well-handled it can do so in a most favourable light, associating you with causes that demonstrate your concern for the public good.

Seizing opportunities

Reactive PR does not have to rely on the media for its effect on the public, or your clients. Outside events can give you an opportunity for comment, in print that you produce yourself.

The outstanding example of this is the Budget; and unlike some events on which you might wish to comment, it is predictable—you can lay your plans well in advance. A short quick commentary, delivered to your clients' desks the morning after the Chancellor's speech, is genuinely useful to them—and magnificent PR for you. It involves very hard work by a large team, extending far into the night, and meticulous organisation is called for, but it can be done. Expanded comment, produced after due consideration, can follow later, and will command more respect than an attempt to be authoritative at short notice.

Other legislation may also give you an opportunity for a similar operation.

The ear of government

It is not only the media that you should cultivate. It is worth fostering contacts with anyone whose opinion counts. People in government, whether national or local, can become valuable sounding boards: you can both sound out opinion in Westminster or County Hall, and ensure that your own point of view does not go by default. An understanding of when, where and how to make effective approaches should be part of a PR consultant's stock in trade.

Backbenchers who lead specialist committees, or are influential in their deliberations, are particularly valuable contacts.

Nurturing such contacts needs to be planned systematically. You can, for example, involve yourself in the 'right' causes, and sponsor the 'right' events. You might consider joining the Industry and Parliament Trust, which exists to improve mutual understanding between legislators and industry. Nothing but good can come of this.

It should perhaps be emphasised that these contacts are not made with the idea of directly generating business, so much as getting your name, your interests, and any special expertise, well to the fore in the minds of the influential. It is, in its way, as important as Press Relations.

Help with recruitment

Public relations also has a contribution to make to recruitment, and again it is achieved by cultivating personal contacts. Your targets will be the University Appointments Boards, people in the Careers Advisory Services, or careers masters and mistresses at schools. For small practices in particular, links with local schools and colleges can be most valuable—and not only for recruitment: schoolboys can go on to become businessmen. Ideally you should involve your most senior people, and also your best students. Make your contacts feel valued and important. Careers advisers welcome facts and detailed briefing; it makes their job easier.

Another aspect of this is the quality of the presentations you make on the 'milk round'. They have a highly critical audience, alert to any hint of the perfunctory or superficial. Once again it is specific *facts*, marshalled in logical order, that will carry conviction. Trouble taken over your presentation will not only pay immediate dividends; it will leave a good impression with people who do not join your firm, but may become important to it in later years.

Recruitment presentations are closely analogous to client presentations. You can treat the former as dry runs for the latter, and use them to polish your act.

Internal Relations

Good PR begins at home. You need a planned programme of staff relations to help your people identify with the firm and understand what you are trying to do. If you are large enough to have a personnel department, this should be one of the most important parts of their remit. Smaller practices can achieve the same result by making internal communication the special responsibility of a partner.

The foundation of this is information. No doubt it is only the larger firms that can afford to run a house magazine; but anyone can produce a duplicated newsletter, once a month or once a quarter. And for important or immediate news there is always the office notice board.

If you do run a house journal it is worth doing it properly, with professional help in the layout and writing—though there is every reason to encourage members of the staff to contribute articles. It must be lively and informative, and edited so as to engage the interest of people at all levels. It should reflect people's external interests as well as the firm's policy.

Another useful vehicle for internal PR is a staff diary. This could include pages of professional data, and also notes about the firm and its services. An internal directory could also be included, giving details of the partners' specialisations; this could be in the form of a loose insert, to allow up-dating more often than once a year.

Keeping in touch

Many of the entrants to the profession who complete their training with you move on elsewhere; but this need not mean that they are lost to you. Not all will go into rival practices. Many will take up accountancy appointments in industry and commerce. And here, if goodwill has been generated and kept alive, they could in course of time become useful allies.

It is worth some effort to keep in touch with your 'alumni', and indeed with past employees in general. If your firm is of a size that makes a house magazine a realistic proposition, you could mail them copies of that. Or an annual directory, giving the whereabouts and positions of former staff, could be sent to them.

Sporting fixtures could be arranged; a refreshment tent might be provided at local or national sporting events, or at agricultural shows, where past and present members and their families and friends could all be welcomed. If they have pleasant memories of their time with you, and respect for your expertise, to keep these green must be good PR.

Do not overlook the value of keeping in touch with your clients. If they are audit clients only, your contact is infrequent, and any plans you may have for expanding your services to them will go better if you keep in touch in the intervals between audits. A client newsletter is one possibility. It could be made into a vehicle for comment on Standards of Recommended Practice, Inflation Accounting or other topics of mutual interest, as well as giving news of developments within the firm.

Objectives, Strategy and Tactics

The objectives and strategy of your PR activities should be exactly the same as for all your other publicity. In other words they should be focussed on fulfilling your marketing strategy.

PR is exactly the same as any other form of publicity, too, in the importance of giving the customers what they want; only in this case the immediate 'customers' are not your clients but the media. What they want is *news*. Above all, they want human-interest news. This is as true of financial journalists as of any others.

Human interest means news of promotions, appointments, moves, successes, attributed views on controversial matters. It also means disagreements, breakaways, failures and *faux pas*. It is not much good trying to suppress the latter category. A cool press release, minimising the matter, is the best course. 'No comment' is actually one of the most eloquent comments of all.

Since PR is so much a people-oriented activity, your tactics depend mainly on fielding the right people. If your marketing strategy is to build on your strengths, and extend existing services into new markets, the people you expose to the media are obviously those that embody the relevant strengths. If it is your taxation service you want to expand, you parade your tax experts.

On the other hand if you have a partner who has special experience of, say, the textile industry, and you have decided that textiles do not have the growth potential to warrant a marketing effort, you will not go to great pains to get articles from his pen into the journals.

Chapter 9

HELP FROM PROFESSIONALS

Even if you had the training and the experience necessary to mount your own publicity, you would hardly have the time. You will need to involve other professionals, both to advise you on the formulation of policy, and to implement the policy once it has been agreed.

The two kinds of professionals whose help and advice you will need are advertising agents and Public Relations consultants. Sometimes you will find them under one roof, and this clearly has a number of advantages: contact is more straightforward and integration of their activities is more easily achieved.

It could be a perfectly sound decision, especially for a smaller firm, not to use paid-for space or air-time, but to rely entirely on Public Relations. In that case you would not need an advertising agent and it becomes irrelevant whether or not the PR consultants you choose are part of an agency or not.

In this chapter we consider how to get the best service from them, starting with a brief explanation of how they operate.

How they earn their money

The central, and rather odd, fact about advertising agencies is rooted far back in history. They were originally agents for the newspapers, earning commission by selling space to advertisers. Not much more than a hundred years ago some of them started to write and design advertisements to fill the space they sold. Thus the modern 'service agency' was tentatively born.

Once this had started it was inevitable that agencies should come to regard themselves as the servants of the advertisers and not of the newspapers, but they continued to take commission from the newspapers. And though many people feel it is anomalous, this remains the normal means of agency remuneration. For a generation or more there have been confident prophecies that a fee system would replace the commission system, but commission shows no sign of fading away, and it can be assumed that it has practical advantages for both advertisers and agencies.

Fees do, however, form a part of the remuneration of most agencies. The standard rate of commission is 15% of the cost of space or air-time; but if the budget allocated to them is small, 15% of it may not be enough to cover the costs the agency incurs in providing a service. A fee may then be negotiated.

It is always open to both agency and client to come to an arrangement whereby commission is rebated in full, and renumeration is wholly by fee, whatever the size of the budget. However, above a certain level, it has been found that the best way of measuring the amount of work involved in servicing an account is by reference to the size of the budget. So in financial terms the end result of fee-based remuneration is not very different from commission.

Certain magazines, mainly trade and technical, pay only 10% commission. In such cases the usual practice is to gross up the charge to the advertiser, so that the agency's remuneration stays at 15% of media costs.

Fifteen per cent commission is also charged on the cost of producing the plates, blocks or litho-negatives from which the newspapers print your advertisements, and the prints sent to television contractors. Producing these is the responsibility of the agency.

Fees are charged for work on non-commissionable items, like booklets. But normally the costs of planning, writing and designing material for commission-paying media are defrayed out of commission, and advertisers do not pay for these aspects of agency service. Since commission is paid only to recognised advertising agencies, you save nothing by trying to do these things yourself. In fact, it would be considerably more costly: in addition to the full 'rate-card' cost of the media, you would have to bear the costs of planning, preparation and production.

Advertising agencies, in spite of being called agents, are principals in law. It is they who pay the media, and them, and only them, that the media can take to court in the event of non-payment.

PR consultancy, by contrast, is paid for wholly on a fee basis, plus any costs incurred.

How an advertising agency is organised

An advertising agency consists of a number of service departments, whose efforts on behalf of each client are co-ordinated by an account director and his assistants. The assistants are called account supervisors or account managers, and may have account executives working under them.

The service departments usually found are Creative, Media and Production. In the Creative Department are found the writers, designers and typographers; sometimes they are organised in groups, each under a Group Head. Always they are headed by a Creative Director, who may or may not be a member of the Board. Confusingly, designers are commonly called Art Directors; this has no bearing at all on their status in the company. 'Visualisers' is another term sometimes used. All these terms are interchangeable.

The Media Department plans how to spend your media budget—in which papers or on which station, how many appearances and in what size or length—and also books the necessary space or air-time. In larger agencies, planning and booking are sometimes handled by separate sections. Booking is not a mechanical operation: it involves considerable skills as 'wheeler and dealer'.

The Production Department is responsible for producing the hardware into which words and pictures have to be translated in order to be reproduced. For papers that print by letter-press—which is virtually all dailies—they have metal 'blocks' made, on which the text and pictures appear in relief. For papers that are lithographically reproduced they generally use film, either positive or negative according to the needs of the paper. This is also the usual requirement of printers for producing booklets. No agency does this work internally; it is invariably entrusted to outside suppliers, specialist production houses who set type, make blocks or produce litho film. The Production Department co-ordinates the work, controls quality and makes sure that the right material gets to the right place at the right time.

Television and radio commercials are generally the responsibility of a separate department in larger agencies. All agencies use specialist production companies; small ones entrust the entire task to them.

There may be other specialist departments: Marketing and Market Research are the most common. And—most important of all from your point of view—some agencies have a PR capability, which may be in a department of the agency or in a subsidiary or sister company.

The account director, who co-ordinates all this activity, is your top-level contact in the agency. He will meet your own senior partners at intervals to discuss overall policy and present his agency's proposals for implementing it. Day-to-day contact with the person charged with immediate responsibility at your end devolves on the account supervisor or manager.

How an agency works

When you have decided on your objective, your strategy and your tactics, it is time to brief the agency on the work you want from it. It is the account director—who in an ideal world has had a hand in working out strategy and tactics—that takes the brief. He will probably be accompanied by the account supervisor, and perhaps the Creative Director or Creative Group Head as well.

This is the start of the process outlined in 'The uses of advertising' and 'What makes effective advertising?'. The end result is a media schedule and creative proposals—typewritten copy and rough layouts—generally accompanied by a written rationale explaining how and why the proposals have been arrived at.

If an illustration is proposed, the layout at this stage almost invariably has a *drawing*—a rough drawing by the visualiser, intended merely to show the position, size and content of the intended picture. It is quite without prejudice as to whether the final illustration will be a drawing or photograph. Occasionally what is called 'scrap art' is used—this is a picture cut out of a magazine, that approximates to the visualiser's intentions. The layout also indicates such things as the area to be occupied by type and the width of the columns, though the type will be represented only by ruled lines. To take photographs and set type are expensive operations, and cannot be undertaken until you have approved the intention.

The media schedule, too, represents at this stage nothing more than a proposal. Nothing has been booked yet.

Almost certainly the copy will need revision, and possibly also the layouts and the media schedule. When they have all been approved, the next stage is set in motion.

The next stage is for 'finished art' to be commissioned. Finished art is what actually appears in the papers by way of illustration. It is almost never produced inside the agency. Instead a freelance photographer or artist, chosen for their skills in the field concerned, are commissioned. At this stage too your approval is sought. You will be able to choose from a large number of photographs, or ask the artist to amend his drawing, but if they have met the agreed brief you cannot ask them to do the job again without paying for it again.

Meanwhile the type is being set. Metal setting, whether by hot-metal or moveable type, is virtually extinct. Almost all advertising copy is now set photographically. What you see after this is not strictly speaking a 'proof' in the conventional sense, but a photocopy of the type matter. You can then make any corrections you feel necessary. If there are mistakes, they are corrected free of charge. If you change your mind at this stage, it can be expensive:

changing one word may necessitate resetting an entire paragraph. The time for changing your mind is when the copy is still in typescript.

When the type is approved, it is pasted up with a print of the photograph or other artwork, to form what is called 'camera-ready artwork'. This shows *exactly* what the advertisement will look like in the papers, and it is your last chance to make changes. From this camera-ready artwork is made the block or film that is sent to the newspapers.

The procedure for producing a booklet is essentially the same, except that no media schedule is involved. When the layout is approved, the agency will get competitive quotes from printers, typesetters and photographers, but remember that these can be adhered to only if the job goes through substantially unchanged—and that changes at proof or artwork stage are disproportionately expensive.

A point to bear in mind about booklets, and indeed about print in general, is that the *origination costs* are the same, however many copies are printed. Origination costs comprise fees for design and writing, finished art and typesetting. They can be a very large proportion of the total cost—in some cases more than half. Consequently the more copies there are, over which the fixed cost can be spread, the lower the unit cost. The difference in cost between 500 and 600 booklets is very much less than 20%.

Proposals for a television commercial are generally presented in the form of a 'story-board', which is a series of drawings rather like the frames of a strip cartoon, showing key stages in the action, and accompanied by a script to describe action and camera movements, and to give the commentary or dialogue. A story-board, unavoidably, has only a tenuous resemblance to the finished article, and approving one cannot be other than an act of faith.

After shooting you will be shown what is called a 'rough cut'. Much more footage will have been shot than is needed for a 30-second commercial, and if you are not happy with what you see, there will be plenty more footage and alternative takes. At this stage there is no sound; that is recorded separately. When you are happy with the rough cut, a 'double head' is made and shown. The picture and the sound-track are still on separate pieces of film, so changes are still easy. But after the double-head has been approved it is not a print that is cut, but the one and only negative, and no more changes are possible.

The final stage that you see is a 'married print'. Then prints are made from the negative and sent out to the contractors. Making a commercial is very expensive, and besides the costs of production you have to reckon with repeat fees for the actors, which reflect the number of times the commercial is transmitted.

While production is going ahead, the approved media schedule is being booked. The final result may differ slightly from what you approved. There may have been problems of availability on particular days and discounts may have been negotiated. But a good agency will ensure that you get at least equivalent value for money—if not better.

There are three critical dates to watch during this process. There is the cancellation date, after which you cannot cancel space or air-time without paying for them; the copy date, which is the latest date on which blocks or film can reach the papers, or prints reach the contractors; and the press date or air-date. It is important not to let your approval procedures become so protracted that the copy date is missed, or you will have to pay for an empty space.

How to use an agency

The time to involve an agency is as early as possible in the planning stage. Most agency directors are well qualified to give marketing advice; and even if you bring in a specialist marketing consultancy, it will help the agency to do good work if they understand the thinking that led to your chosen strategy.

It is a cardinal principle to take your agency fully into your confidence. They cannot work effectively unless they know everything about you. If you are selective about what you tell them, you are in effect pre-empting one of the most valuable things your agency can do for you—looking at your firm from an outsider's point of view and selecting the facts that are going to make your claims credible. You are too close to your firm and its services to do this effectively yourself.

But there is more to it than this. The fact is that mutual trust is the only basis for a satisfactory relationship between client and agency. Once this has been eroded the relationship is best terminated.

The personal chemistry must be right. If you find you do not have a rapport with the account supervisor or executive assigned to work with you, do not suffer in silence. Go to the top of the agency and ask for a change of team. So too with the creative team. They can always be changed if you do not get on, and it is a lot less agonising than changing your agency.

If you have complaints, air them. Do not let them fester. It is more than likely that if they are brought to the attention of the agency management they will be put right. If they are not, you probably have the wrong agency.

It is best to appoint one person to be responsible for all your advertising, and to empower him or her to take decisions. You do not get good results if everything has to be decided by a committee. A camel, they say in the advertising business, is a horse designed by a committee.

It would be astonishing if you always approved instantly every 'creative' proposal put in front of you. But it is extremely discouraging to the creative team if all you say is 'I don't like it'. Our chapter, 'What makes effective advertising', is intended to help you to criticise constructively. Try to say what it is that you think is wrong.

If the agency always agrees with you, their professionalism must fall under suspicion. (You probably know the story about the client who asks what time it is, to which the account executive replies 'What time would you like it to be, J B?'.) The situation is the same if the creative team mounts a high horse when its work is criticised. Professionals should be prepared to argue for their solutions to your problems—politely, of course, but firmly and rationally. And naturally this involves listening with an open mind to *your* arguments.

The argument should revolve around whether the proposal meets the brief, and not around personal taste or the creative ego. Advertisements should be criticised—and defended—solely on whether or not they efficiently communicate what readers or viewers want to know.

It is also necessary to issue a warning against allowing subjective judgments to colour one's attitude to a proposed media schedule. The fact that you may detest the *Guardian*—or the *Telegraph*—is not a good reason for excluding it from the schedule if the facts indicate that your target audience read it in large numbers. But it does sometimes happen.

Your relationship with your agency should be an exclusive one while it lasts. You will not get good work out of them if they are continually looking over their shoulder at some other agency. And it is best if the relationship is seen as a long term one.

How to choose an agency

The important thing in choosing an agency is to choose the *people*—you must feel happy about the prospect of working with them for a number of years.

Look at their work. See if you like the way they have solved other people's problems. See if you like their style. Get them to talk about themselves and their approach to advertising. Find out what their existing clients think of them—nobody minds you doing this. Do they understand your business and your professional ethics, and the rules that govern your publicity?

How do you start looking, though?

You can start by considering how large an agency you want. Do you want a big West End agency, with a wealth of sophisticated services, or a small shop to whom you will be an important client? Many agencies have a threshold appropriation below which they will not take you on. Others may consider clients spending less than this if they are willing to pay a fee. You do not have to go to London. There are many excellent agencies in the provinces, including many small ones eager to grow bigger; and whose 'threshold' appropriation is likely to be lower than that of a large agency, especially a London one. At the most modest level of all, there are a number of individuals working as freelance consultants, writers or designers; they should be able to help you put together a booklet and produce local advertising. A local printer may be able to put you in touch; or he may offer a design service himself. If he does, it would be as well to get a second opinion on it.

When you have thought about this you can talk about your needs to the Institute of Practitioners in Advertising, or to the PR Register or to the Advertising Agency Register, who will show you the work of agencies appropriate to your needs and size, and put you in touch. They make no charge to advertisers for this. The Advertiser's Annual ('The Blue Book') may also give you some useful leads.

You may already be using an agency for recruitment advertising. If it is one that specialises in recruitment, it would be unwise to assume that they are competent to handle your practice advertising—though they may represent themselves as capable of doing so. If they are part of a large general advertising group, and you are happy with their service, it could be worthwhile looking at another agency in the group.

Or, of course, you may know someone who has experience of agencies and can steer you in the right direction.

The worst way of choosing an agency is to ask a number of them to prepare proposals on a competitive, speculative basis. Even if you are going to be a big enough spender to tempt agencies to undertake this very expensive operation, it is not a good plan. The inevitable result will be that the agencies will produce advertising that they think you will like, not what they think will solve your problems.

For one thing, they do not know you well enough to gauge your ability to recognise the solution to your problem when you see it. They have a suspicion that non-advertising people judge advertising according to whether the agency that produced it is successful or not. And are you sure they are wrong?

What sort of agency?

Broadly speaking there are two kinds of agency: consumer and specialist. Consumer agencies are those whose clients market consumer goods, often on very large budgets. Specialist agencies concentrate on a particular segment of advertising: recruitment, industrial goods, agricultural supplies or pharmaceuticals, for example. As far as accountants are concerned, 'specialist' means 'financial'. There are a number of agencies specialising in financial advertising, which can embrace anything whatever to do with money.

Should you choose a financial agency or a consumer one? There is no reason in principle why you have to go to a financial agency just because you are accountants. There is something to be said on both sides.

Consumer agencies have a reputation—often well deserved—for creativity. It is certainly true that they tend to attract the younger creative writers and designers, because they offer more opportunity for the conspicuous display of talent. In particular they offer work on television, which is what all creative people crave.

If you feel that striking and dramatic advertising is what you need, then consider a consumer agency. But there are two warnings to sound. The first is that you will have to devote much more time and effort to briefing them, and even then it may be some time before you can feel confident that they have really understood your problems and can handle financial ideas with a sure touch. The other is that the brightest creative sparks may despise 'mere' financial work, and that you will find yourself working with the Second XI.

A financial agency should have no difficulty in getting to grips with your problems. Its people should already have a grasp of the concepts involved, and be skilled in communicating ideas about money. Moreover many of its staff, especially on the creative staff, will have a background in consumer advertising. But it is unlikely that its work will be that which most strikes you when you are looking at specimens and show-reels. And, since even the largest financial agency is much smaller than a large consumer agency, it may not command the same resources in, for example, research.

(Unless, as is often the case, it is a subsidiary of a large consumer agency.)

A further point to bear in mind is that there are very few financial agencies outside London.

What a PR consultancy can do for you

If your PR consultants are part of your advertising agency, it is a good idea to brief them at the same time as the advertising team since much the same considerations will govern the planning they do for you. They too will need to understand your strategy and know all there is to know about your firm and its capabilities.

According to what you wish to achieve, they will identify the journalists who can be most useful to you, and begin to arrange the necessary contacts. It is the consultants' business to know the press thoroughly and to be on close terms with its key people. In collaboration with you they will work out a programme of lunch-time meetings of the kind described in an earlier chapter. Thus the groundwork for successful PR is laid.

They have the contacts with editors that can help to get signed articles by your partners into the press. They know the people at the local TV and Radio stations, and can prepare the ground for your top people to become involved in programmes. They can arrange for your partners to be schooled in the art of making a good impression on the air; but it is your spokesmen's knowledge and articulacy, and nothing else, that gets the invitation to appear. Your consultants can arrange a meeting, but it is up to your side to see that it is a meeting of minds.

It will normally be the consultants that draft and distribute press releases.

They can initiate contacts with influential members of committees, whether in Parliament or local government, to foster understanding of your needs—and of the importance of the contribution you make to society.

They will identify, in the light of your strategy, suitable activities for you to sponsor (if you agree that this is a desirable tactic); and they attend to the administration, and the liaison with the organisation whose activity you are sponsoring.

They will be able to advise you on how to react to sudden media interest in your activities; they can help you put together your milk-round presentation; and they will do most of the work on a house-magazine, if you have one. They can find someone to do the editing, and arrange for design and printing, either through the agency to which they are linked or through one of the companies that specialise in this work.

A press-cutting service is offered by most consultancies. They will monitor the press and send you cuttings of items on any topic you specify: your own firm, the profession as a whole, accountancy techniques, the economy . . . the cost depends on the range of subjects and newspapers you want covered.

If it is the case that you are not going to undertake any advertising, and consequently do not need an agency, PR consultants should be able to help you to get booklets produced. Some of the bigger consultancies have in-house writers and designers. All have links with outside people who can write and design, and also with printers. They should be able to assemble a team whose talents will match your needs.

There is, in fact, considerable overlap between the peripheral services offered by PR consultancies and those of advertising agencies. Both can help with the writing, design and printing of booklets and house journals; both can help you devise presentations. But a PR consultancy would have to work through an agency in order to place advertisements; and an agency would not have the contacts with the editorial side of the media that a PR consultancy offers.

Chapter 10

WHAT DO OTHER PROFESSIONS DO?

Accountancy is not the only profession venturing into the more competitive world of which advertising is part. Indeed the medical professions are now the only ones still to forbid it totally, and it is difficult to imagine any government legislating so as to put doctors, surgeons and dentists in a position where they would be obliged to advertise.

In the middle of 1984 the Royal College of Veterinary Surgeons accepted advertising in principle, 'subject to certain restraints'; and the Law Society also decided that solicitors should be allowed to advertise.

Hitherto solicitors have been allowed only 'visiting card' advertisements; the information they contained would not have helped a member of the public seeking a solicitor with experience relevant to his particular needs. Now only TV advertising, direct mail and comparisons with rivals are banned.

Architects were until recently as restricted as any profession, but they now have more latitude than accountants. The rules as to content are much the same, but direct mail is allowed and there are no size limitations on newspaper space. The relaxation is too recent to allow any generalisations about its effects.

There is not, therefore, a great deal of experience in this country of the nature or results of advertising by the professions, and it is only from stockbrokers that there is anything to be learned—though, as will be seen, not very much.

Stockbrokers have had limited freedom to advertise for a number of years, and The Stock Exchange Council allows them factual descriptions of their service and their specialisations.

This should give them all the freedom they need to produce effective advertising. But the profession was not quick to take advantage of this, and it is obviously pertinent to enquire why.

The main reason seems to be a perfectly valid marketing one. Most of the big firms have identified their target market as the institutional investors. This is a very small market numerically, and media advertising would be a wasteful way of attacking it. There is also a strong feeling that advertising would be ineffective against this audience (which may be mistaken) and that there are more effective means of getting business (which may well be true). Private clients are another matter: advertising is rightly seen as a good way of reaching them. See *Figure 18*.

Stockbrokers rely heavily on personal recommendations by satisfied clients to dissatisfied clients of other brokers. They feel that the best way of getting new business is to establish a reputation for reliability, integrity and good dealing with existing clients, and that this reputation will spread—and is what brings in business. There is a good deal of anecdotal evidence to support this. It features not only the after-lunch telephone call from one institution to another, but the institutional dealer who moves to a responsible position in another institution, taking with him a regard for the broker he has been dealing with.

It is likely that this situation will change with the imminent abolition of minimum commission rules. We are already seeing much more use of advertising by stockbrokers; they are finding they have no choice.

Production of brochures as a means of winning business is much more widespread, though some of the biggest firms have never had one. Their effect is difficult to evaluate. They seem to us to be short on fact and long on unsupported claims; but they cannot be intended to work on their own. Seen as an adjunct to a personal visit, they may make a contribution. This is always a possible way of using brochures, and more economical than widespread distribution.

Because of the nature of the marketing problems facing stockbrokers, their experience is not very relevant to accountants.

There are a number of occupations that might be described as semi-professions. They have professional institutes, that issue codes of conduct and in some cases oversee professional education and award diplomas. But there has never been any bar on members advertising. And there is, in many cases, no legal bar to non-members engaging in the business. Since this is the direction in which accountancy seems to be moving, it is worth considering what, in practice, such businesses do about advertising.

Advertising itself is an interesting example, though an anomalous one because of its system of remuneration. (It is really professional status that lies at the heart of the argument about fees versus commission.) But since they stand to their clients essentially in the relation of professional advisers, it seems legitimate to include advertising agencies in this survey.

Figure 18 An example of stockbrokers' advertising

The curious thing is how little advertising is done by advertising agencies for their own services—and the fact that most of what there is appears in their own trade press. It is also striking that much of it is not very good. For this there are perhaps two reasons: that since everyone in an agency is an expert, every advertisement is a camel—produced by a committee; and further, that the really good agencies do not need to advertise. The reason for this is that their products are extremely visible, and moreover with their quality apparent for all to see. There is no packaging (except to the extent that a superbly designed advertisement may have nothing to say), and it is easy to find out who is responsible for any particular advertisement.

Clearly this does not apply to accountancy firms, the results of whose efforts are seldom visible.

Insurance brokers are in a somewhat similar position: they give what is supposed to be impartial professional advice, but everyone recognises that it is in fact coloured by the commissions they receive (which is not, on the whole, true of advertising agencies, since their commissions are standardised). Insurance brokers spend large sums on advertising; it is impossible to open a quality national newspaper without finding advertisements for the financial planning services they offer. It is impossible to generalise about their advertising: the content varies widely and the quality is very uneven. We reproduce some examples as *Figure 19*.

The clearing banks are interesting hybrids in this respect. The local bank manager is losing—or perhaps abandoning—his traditional role of financial adviser, but this is being taken up by head office departments of the banks, or by subsidiary companies: they all now have trust departments, or trust companies, dispensing investment advice, a tax service and trustee services, and often acting as insurance brokers. These activities all represent a competitive threat to accountancy firms, even without the banks' growing involvement in accounting as such.

They do not do a great deal of media advertising for these services, though Barclaytrust was launched with quite a substantial press campaign. But they engage in a great deal of publicity, of a very economical kind. They confine their marketing effort almost entirely to their own customers, and publicity is mainly in the form of 'account stuffers'—folders and booklets that are mailed to customers in the same envelope as their monthly statements. So long as they have a low uptake of these services by their customers, this is good marketing, and much of the material is of high quality. Some of it is reproduced as *Figure 20*.

The clearing banks have a number of advantages that give them a flying start—mainly the fact that they have high visibility. They

Figure 19a Some examples of insurance brokers' advertising. We leave it to you to decide which are good and which bad.

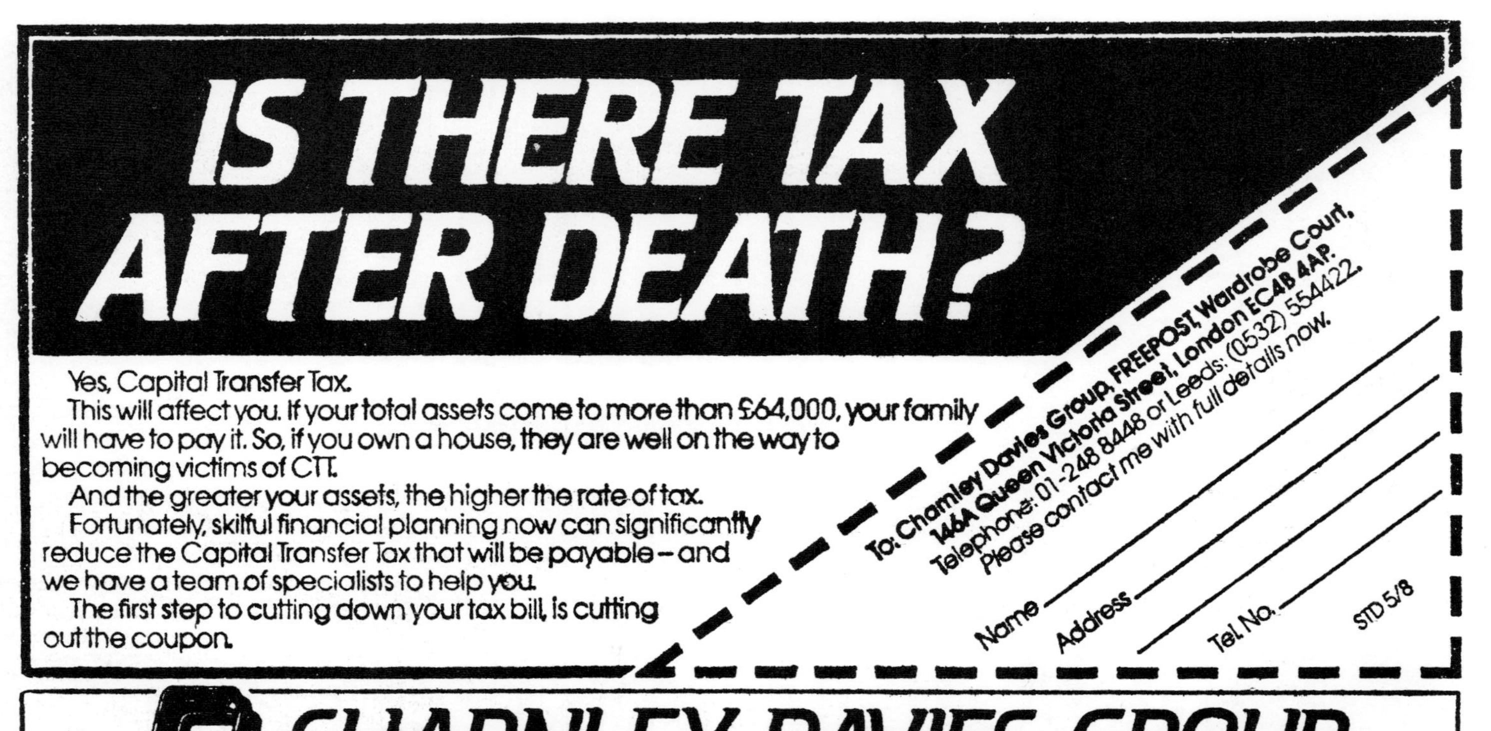
IS THERE TAX AFTER DEATH?
Yes, Capital Transfer Tax.
This will affect you. If your total assets come to more than £64,000, your family will have to pay it. So, if you own a house, they are well on the way to becoming victims of CTT.
And the greater your assets, the higher the rate of tax.
Fortunately, skilful financial planning now can significantly reduce the Capital Transfer Tax that will be payable – and we have a team of specialists to help you.
The first step to cutting down your tax bill, is cutting out the coupon.
To: Charnley Davies Group, FREEPOST, Wardrobe Court, 146A Queen Victoria Street, London EC4B 4AP.
Telephone: 01-248 8448 or Leeds: (0532) 554422.
Please contact me with full details now.
Name
Address
Tel. No.
STD 5/8
CHARNLEY DAVIES GROUP
Members of National Association of Security and Investment Managers. Members of the British Insurance Brokers' Association.

Figure 19b

BECOME AN INTERNATIONAL INVESTOR for only £30 a month

Why save with a bank or building society when, for as little as £30 a month, your money can be invested world-wide by one of the City's top investment management teams?

A new 5-year savings plan is now available which almost certainly offers the best value-for-money in the market. And it incorporates the following benefits:–

★ Investment in a Fund that, since the launch in April 1982, has achieved an average annual growth rate of *more than 22%* (while a building society share account has grown at 6.75%).

★ A *valuable bonus* at the end of years 3, 4 and 5.

★ The full accumulated cash sum can be drawn ***free of tax*** by basic rate taxpayers in 5 years' time.

★ *Tax-free income* option at the end of 5 years.

★ Life assurance cover is included.

★ Early cash-in facility, with no deductions.

You owe it to yourself to find out more about this exceptional plan today.

N.B. It should be remembered that the value of the units allocated to your plan may go down from time to time as well as up. While past performance cannot necessarily be taken as a guide to the future, the skills of the management group involved are clearly well above average.

To **Reed Stenhouse Gibbs**, 10 Grosvenor Gardens,
FREEPOST, London SW1W 0BR (no stamp required). Tel: 01-730 8221.

Please contact me with details of this exceptional value savings plan.

Name ____________________

Address ____________________

____

County ____________ Tel. No: ____________

Present Income £ ________ Date of Birth ________ Tax Rate ______%

Amount available for regular savings £ ____________ per year/month

Lump sum amount available for investment £ ____________

Licensed Dealer in Securities.
Group established in 1904. 197 offices in 35 countries.
Registered in Edinburgh No. 47984 546PA 29/7

REED STENHOUSE GIBBS

Figure 19c

RETIREMENT PLANNING
(Free Booklet)

MAXIMUM AGE 85
GUARANTEED INCOME

10% to 13%+!*

(Free of basic rate tax)
PAID ANUALLY/MONTHLY
(Through major Financial Institutions)
Send now for quotation without obligation

Flexible Investment Planning Ltd., Freepost, Urmston, Manchester M31 2HX. Tel.: 061 747 7054 or 061 748 1554

Name ST2

Address ....

....

Age .... Tel. No ....

Married/Single .... Tax Rate ....%

Amount for investment £...
* According to age and quotation selected

FLEXIBLE INVESTMENT PLANNING LIMITED

Figure 19d

Figure 20 'Account stuffers', advertising the financial services of the clearing banks, are often of high quality.

Hambros Bank Limited

Hambros is active in sponsoring new issues on the Unlisted Securities Market and in providing specialist advice to companies that wish to consider joining this market. The following companies have already been introduced to the Unlisted Securities Market by Hambros:

Airship Industries Limited
Bespak plc
Dewey Warren Holdings PLC
Jebsens Drilling P.L.C.
Mebon plc
Mnemos, Limited
Moray Firth Maltings plc
Sovereign Oil & Gas PLC
Tunstall Telecom Group Plc

Hambros also offers a full range of corporate finance advice and other merchant banking services to companies already dealt in on the USM and through the Official List.

Hambros Bank Limited,
Corporate Finance Department,
41 Bishopsgate, London EC2P 2AA.
Telephone: 01-588 2851.

Figure 21 Merchant bank advertising. Much of it consists of glorified 'visiting cards', but there is some selling of specific financial services.

have high-street branches everywhere, and spend large sums on advertising their current account services (especially to the young), and their unit trusts.

Merchant banks do not have high visibility, but they have great prestige—of which their advertising shows them keenly conscious. Few of their services are directly competitive with yours, and they are a useful source of referrals rather than rivals. However, their advertising has some points of interest for accountants. It seems to consist largely of glorified 'visiting card' advertisements, very like those to which our own profession has hitherto been restricted, but larger. They can hardly have pulled many enquiries. Since there are no restraints on what a merchant bank may do by way of advertising, this is clearly a self-imposed restriction. It may derive from a sense of what is due to their dignity: more probably is due to the fact that much of it appears in special supplements or surveys, where the banks wish to establish a presence, but not to incur much trouble or expense. To attract enquiries is not the object. It seems, nevertheless, a waste of opportunity.

Merchant banks get some 'name publicity' when they act as lead underwriters in a bond issue, and what is aptly known as a 'tombstone' advertisement appears as a matter of record. Their most valuable media publicity, however, is probably derived from the prominence of their name in the prospectuses of offers for sale.

An example of a merchant bank's advertising is shown as *Figure 21*, which includes some genuinely 'selling' advertisements featuring specific services.

Our last example is for a firm describing itself as 'Accountants and Investment Consultants'. It appeared in October 1983, and we reproduce it without comment.

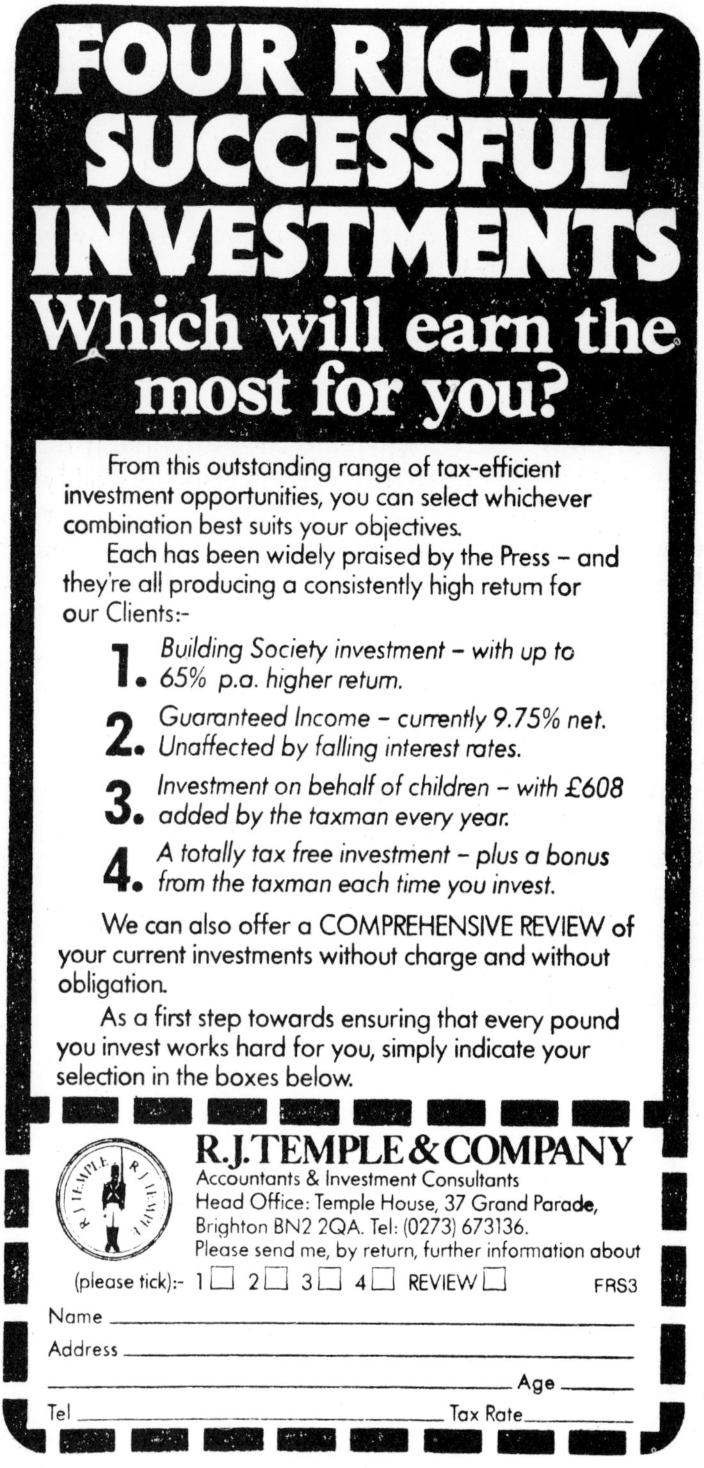

FOUR RICHLY SUCCESSFUL INVESTMENTS

Which will earn the most for you?

From this outstanding range of tax-efficient investment opportunities, you can select whichever combination best suits your objectives.

Each has been widely praised by the Press – and they're all producing a consistently high return for our Clients:-

1. *Building Society investment – with up to 65% p.a. higher return.*
2. *Guaranteed Income – currently 9.75% net. Unaffected by falling interest rates.*
3. *Investment on behalf of children – with £608 added by the taxman every year.*
4. *A totally tax free investment – plus a bonus from the taxman each time you invest.*

We can also offer a COMPREHENSIVE REVIEW of your current investments without charge and without obligation.

As a first step towards ensuring that every pound you invest works hard for you, simply indicate your selection in the boxes below.

R.J.TEMPLE & COMPANY
Accountants & Investment Consultants
Head Office: Temple House, 37 Grand Parade,
Brighton BN2 2QA. Tel: (0273) 673136.
Please send me, by return, further information about

(please tick):- 1☐ 2☐ 3☐ 4☐ REVIEW☐ FRS3

Name ______

Address ______

______ Age ______

Tel ______ Tax Rate ______

Figure 22

Chapter 11

THE AMERICAN EXPERIENCE

Only ten years ago, the attitude of the American accountancy bodies to advertising was even more restrictive than ours. It was Federal pressure that led to relaxation. In 1977 virtually all restrictions, except for a ban on direct solicitation, were lifted. In 1978 even the ban on solicitation went. It was to all intents and purposes a free-for-all, governed only by the AICPA's rule 502: 'a member shall not seek to obtain clients by advertising or other form of solicitation in a manner that is false, misleading or deceptive'. This neatly summarises Britain's Code of Advertising Practice.

American experience is therefore highly relevant.

Rather as in the case of stockbrokers in this country, advertising agencies have not grown rich at accountants' expense. Neither the hoardings nor the air-waves have been inundated.

'Advertising hasn't caused that much change', says a partner in a San Francisco accountancy firm. 'Conservative fears have not been realised; there has been no huge and sustained advertising activity.'

The first thing that happened was a burst of advertising by the big firms. They ran nationwide campaigns in magazines like *Time* and *Fortune*: full-page advertisements, many in colour. It was of course extremely expensive, and even the biggest firms could not keep it up for long.

Some trends have caused concern. An article in *The Accountant*, for 18 August 1983, describes 'block type advertisements that are catchy and trendy rather than informative: "Do you think others get a better break than you on income tax? Come and see John Smith CPA" '. There is, reports *The Accountant*, a move to ban direct, uninvited soliciting; but legal advice is that, if such a ban were challenged in the courts, it would be overthrown.

Although solicitation has caused much hard feeling, the profession seems, on the whole, to have settled down with advertising very well. A member of AICPA's ethics committee says, 'The way advertising has worked out is a tribute to the profession. Accountants are not hucksters nor salesmen, and they have handled advertising carefully . . . The restraints of good taste and dignity have worked.'

It is possible to quarrel with this pronouncement. Practice development demands that every accountant should be a salesman. And to handle advertising carefully is not incompatible with salesmanship; some would say it is an essential qualification for it. But it is true that 'the restraints of good taste and dignity have worked'. *Figures 23* to *25* show some of the results.

Firms large and small are finding advertising a useful weapon against the developing threat of the 'financial supermarket', which is much closer in the USA than it is here. There, banks are buying up stockbroking firms, and stockbroking firms are merging with insurance brokers. In Britain, the changes on The Stock Exchange have already initiated a move in the same direction.

Small firms in particular are finding advertising an effective defence against competition from non-accountants. *The Accountant* reports that they are using television as well as newspapers to advertise their taxation and book-keeping services to small businesses, in markets that they would otherwise find it difficult to reach. Second-tier firms are using advertising vigorously to defend what they regard as their territory—the small-business market—against encroachment by the big practices.

It has to be remembered that, in America, television coverage is very much more fragmented than here. There are many more stations, some of them covering quite small populations. Going on television is not, therefore, quite the financial commitment is is here.

'The big firms', continues *The Accountant*, 'keep their names before the public by studies of economic problems, which are released to the business press. They give radio interviews and are seen to be knowledgeable on the issues of the day.' In short, they make good use of the techniques of Public Relations.

The CPA Marketing Report wrote in August 1983 that most firms seemed to be 'stepping up seminar and publication activity and beefing up marketing staffs'. Co-operative seminars are beginning to appear, run in conjunction with representatives from other industries, mainly those in which the accountancy sponsor specialises.

It seems to be a common experience that advertising is most effective in generating taxation business. This is not surprising: help with taxation is by far the commonest accountancy need throughout society. Firms have found that they need to train staff to log and evaluate response and respond to leads. This is something that firms in this country could usefully bear in mind. Much money has been wasted by inexperienced advertisers for lack of such training.

It is interesting to note that in spite of their longer experience with advertising, American accountants can make the kind of mistake against which we cautioned in our section on Relevance. *Figure 23* shows an advertisement on which the President of a New York advertising agency commented, 'Unfortunately the headline . . . is guaranteed to attract little attention. And it should be remembered that 80% of people never read beyond the headline . . . Price Waterhouse is giving away a free booklet on automobile expenses and benefits. So why doesn't the headline say that?'

By contrast, the Deloittes advertisement (*Figure 24*) and the Alexander Grant advertisement (*Figure 25*) go straight to the point, and say clearly what the deal is.

It seems that, in America, the profession has not only learned to live with advertising, but is finding out its positive aspects.

Better than just tinkering around

Price Waterhouse has prepared a handy booklet, Automobile Expenses and Benefits, which outlines the basic tax facts about using an automobile for business.

The booklet explains how tax rules apply to both employers and employees, and to professionals and business owners. In addition to telling you how some arrangements can be more tax effective than others, the booklet provides forms to help in calculating deductible automobile expenses.

Information on a special computer program to compare leasing or buying your company's automobiles can also be obtained from any member of the firm's tax section.

To obtain a copy of Automobile Expenses and Benefits, please contact your nearest Price Waterhouse office or call Maureen Feeheley at our National Distribution Centre in Toronto, (416) 863-1133.

Figures 23 to 25 Some examples of accountants' advertising from the United States.

What Should I Be Doing Now To Take My Company Public?

As a first step you can get some answers from the professionals at Deloitte Haskins & Sells who specialize in advising entrepreneurs on raising growth capital.

Take our booklets, *Strategies for Going Public,* and *Raising Venture Capital.* They can give you a good understanding of the entire process.

For example, consider what you can learn from our latest booklet, the one on "...Going Public."

You'll find out about business plans, and how to write them... as well as the criteria you should use to decide whether to go public at all. You'll learn about alternative strategies for raising growth capital... the registration statement, and the whole registration process.

To get answers like these, and to receive our booklets send in the coupon below.

Or call Jan Grayson at (312) 861-1161.

☐ Send me Strategies for Going Public.
☐ Send me Raising Venture Capital
☐ Call me to discuss my business.

Name ______________________

Company ______________________

Title ____________ Telephone ____________

Address ______________________

City, State, Zip ______________________

Deloitte Haskins+Sells
CHICAGO

200 East Randolph
Chicago, Illinois 60601

Figure 24

CONGRATULATIONS. YOUR PRESENT ACCOUNTING SYSTEM CAN NO LONGER KEEP UP.

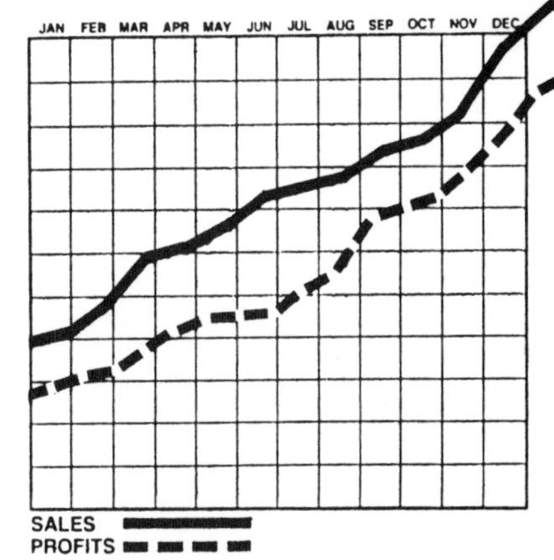

Your company is exhibiting the classic signs of growth. Sales are up. Profits are up.

And your accounting department can no longer keep up.

That's where we can help. At Alexander Grant, we've been helping growing companies grow for over 60 years.

When you work with us, you'll have the backing of one of the country's largest CPA firms. And you'll work with a team of specialists that doesn't just have business experience. But has experience with your business.

We've even put our experience into a microcomputer accounting system. The first ever offered by an accounting firm.

It easily handles general ledger, order entry and purchases. As well as payroll and inventory.

We'll install it. Make sure everyone knows how to use it. And be there for any follow-up you'll need in the future.

Once it's in, you'll have instant access to information. The right information. In the right place. In the right form.

You'll be able to keep track of profits, cash flow and how your salespeople are doing.

You'll even get current financial statements while they're still current.

To learn more, just send in the coupon. Or call Wayne Hamilton at (415) 986-3900.

He'll tell you about all the ways we can help your company as it grows.

And grows.

And grows.

Send to Alexander Grant, One California Street, Suite 2100, San Francisco, CA 94111.

☐ Please tell me more about your microcomputer system.
☐ Please tell me more about your other business services.

Name ____
Title ____
Company ____
Address ____ City ____
State ____ Zip ____ Phone ____

Alexander Grant
We help growing companies grow.

Figure 25

Chapter 12

CONCLUSION

Where substantial sums of money are involved, the most effective advertising is sober, informative and factual. Not razzmatazz but relevance is what gets the message home. There is nothing here that anybody need feel is undignified or unbecoming a professional man or woman.

Moreover, the more factual your advertising is, the less need there is to resort to generalisations, which are generally more or less boastful and always less than convincing. Good advertising has nothing to do with boasting.

Successful advertising need not involve enormous expenditure. It does involve meticulous planning. Unless you get the basics right you will be thrashing around in the dark. You must be quite clear about your marketing objective, and the strategy and tactics you pursue to get there. Publicity is simply the weapon you use in your tactical marketing activities. It is always the servant of marketing, never an activity conducted for its own sake.

With the marketing strategy right, you will be able to work out a media plan that brings your message to the right people, at the right time, in the most cost-effective way possible. And you will know *what* you should be saying to them. How you should say it will, we hope, be a little clearer when you have read this book.

Public Relations is best used in conjunction with advertising. But if financial constraints force you to choose one or the other, your choice must be guided by a careful evaluation of how well each will work to further your marketing goals. And PR, no less than advertising, demands careful planning in the light of those goals.

In the days of the Raj, the Government of India had a one-word motto: 'Thorough'. We commend it to you.

For immediate release

PUBLICITY AND ADVERTISING: NEW RULES FOR CHARTERED ACCOUNTANTS

At its meeting today (1 August) the Council of the Institute of Chartered Accountants in England and Wales agreed a revision of the sections of the members' Guide to Professional Ethics dealing with publicity and advertising. The new guidance has been developed in agreement with the Irish and Scottish Institutes of Chartered Accountants, and the three bodies are to publish statements and Explanatory Notes of identical effect.

The essence of the new guidance will be to permit individual members and firms to advertise their services in the national press and on radio and television for the first time.

The main changes to the Guide are to the Statements which regulate members' conduct on *Advertising and Publicity* and on *Obtaining Professional Work*. The revision will result in consequential amendments to other parts of the Ethical Guide: copies of all the new guidance are available from the Institute and will be published in full in the September issue of *Accountancy*.

The new guidance comes into effect on 1 October 1984 and the present rules remain in force until then. Members will be expected not to anticipate the formal introduction of the new provisions of the Ethical Guide.

Copies of the revised statements and Explanatory Notes on *Publicity and Advertising*, and on *Obtaining Professional Work* are attached.

Press enquiries to: A J Hardcastle, President of the Institute
A W Moore, Secretary, Professional Conduct
J Maurice, Under-Secretary, Professional Conduct

Telephone: 01–628 7060

Note to editors
Professional Practice Announcements by members in local newspapers have been permitted since October 1981.

STATEMENT 3
PUBLICITY FOR AND ADVERTISING OF PROFESSIONAL SERVICES

General

1 A member preparing or authorising the issue of material falling within this Statement should do so with a due sense of responsibility to the profession and to the public as a whole. In particular, *such material should be in good taste both as to content and presentation and should not belittle services offered by others, whether members or not, either by claiming superiority for the services of a particular member or otherwise*. The same attitude should be adopted towards activities mentioned in subsequent paragraphs.

2 Additionally, members who advertise should have in mind the requirements of the Advertising Standards Authority as to legality, decency, honesty and truthfulness.

3 Members should always have regard to the requirements of Statement 7.

Publicity

4 Publicity for members is acceptable.

Advertising

5 A member may advertise his services to the public.

6 To safeguard new entrants to the market and the competitive position of all firms regardless of their financial resources, *advertisements should in size and scale be related to a requirement to inform rather than to impress.* In pursuance of this principle *advertisements in all newspapers should not exceed 1/4 of a page;* nor should advertisements by associated firms appearing in the same edition of a newspaper exceed in total that limit. *Whilst specific limitations are not prescribed for advertisements appearing in media other than newspapers, similar restraint should be observed.*

7 *Advertisements may refer to the basis on which fees are calculated; however, the inclusion in an advertisement of hourly or other charging rates could be misleading and is not permissible.*

8 A member may also advertise:
  (a) for staff, a partnership, salaried employment or for subcontract work;
  (b) on behalf of a client;
  (c) in a fiduciary or other capacity;
  (d) members' appointments, the opening of a new office, changes in the membership of a firm and changes in the name, address or telephone number of a firm.

Directories

9 A member may be listed in any directory whether printed or available through some other medium of communication.

Literature

10 Professional literature written or published by members, whether technical or descriptive of the services provided by the member, may be provided free to clients and to those who ask for it. It should not, however, be sent unsolicited to non-clients.

Sponsorship

11 A member's contribution to good causes, whether by way of donation or sponsorship, may be suitably and publicly acknowledged by the recipient. Appropriate causes for support include registered charities, education, sport and the arts. Members in doubt as to whether a prospective recipient falls within the above categories or wishing to venture outside them should, in good time, consult with the Ethics Committee.

Exhibitions and seminars

12 A member may participate in exhibitions, seminars and similar activities.

EXPLANATORY NOTES ON STATEMENT 3

Good taste

1 Publicity and advertising material prepared or authorised by members must be consistent with the dignity of a profession.

2 Judgment as to what may or may not constitute good taste can only be made in the context of the particular facts on which that judgment is exercised. It is possible, however, to give some broad guidance and general examples as to what might, in appropriate circumstances, be regarded as not according with good taste. Thus material which tends to sensationalise or shock, or which is likely to give offence to religious beliefs, or is racist, is unacceptable. Other possible examples include the trivialisation of important issues, excessive reliance on a particular personality or personalities, the deriding of public figures, the disparagement of educational attainment and material which makes odious comparisons or is strident in tone, hectoring or extravagant.

Literature

3 Technical literature written or published by members of the Institute may be provided, unsolicited, to educational establishments, public libraries and other professional bodies. It may also be sent for review in publications with an interest in the subject matter of its content.

STATEMENT 7
OBTAINING PROFESSIONAL WORK

1 A member should not in any circumstances obtain or seek professional work for himself or another member in an unprofessional manner.

2 *In particular, a member should not obtain or seek professional work by direct mailing or by the practice commonly referred to as 'cold calling'.*

3 A practising member should not give any commission, fee or reward to a third party, not being either his employee or another public accountant, in return for the introduction of a client.

4 A member who is an employee, other than an employee of a public accountant, should not, on behalf of his employer, carry on in his own name or in partnership any business which is normally carried on by a public accountant.

EXPLANATORY NOTES ON STATEMENT 7

Cold calling

1 Cold calling is the act of making or instigating an unsolicited approach to a non client with a view to obtaining professional work. It includes the act of making an appointment to call or making overtures by telephone or by letter.

Direct mailing

2 Subject to what is said in paragraph 3 below, direct mailing and the sending of unsolicited circulars, brochures or other literature about the firm to non clients of the firm are forms of cold calling.

Contact with others

3 A member may inform others engaged in the provision of financial services to the public in the same locality of the services he himself can offer.

4 A member may invite holders of public office, as well as others

engaged in the provision of financial services to the public, to attend specific events of relevance and importance to the community they serve.

Work for other organisations

5 There are many cases in which members in practice are retained by organisations which, in their turn, offer advice to their members on accountancy matters. The member retained by the organisation may, in relation to matters referred to him by the organisation, deal only with the organisation itself and not directly with any of its members. The member should ensure that any literature issued by the organisation in which his name or the name of his firm is mentioned conforms to the guidelines contained in Statement 3.

INDEX